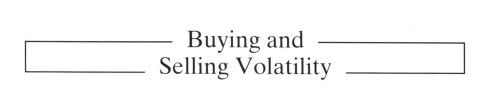

Buying and
Selling Volatility

Wiley Frontiers in Finance

Series Editor   Edward I. Altman, New York University

Buying and Selling Volatility

Kevin B. Connolly

JOHN WILEY & SONS

Chichester • New York • Weinheim • Brisbane • Singapore • Toronto

Note on the queries regarding the use of the disk:

Please contact Professor Connolly by fax on 01737 830373 directly and not the publishers.

Other Wiley Editorial Offices

John Wiley & Sons, Inc., 605 Third Avenue,
New York, NY 10158-0012, USA

Weinheim • Brisbane • Singapore • Toronto

Library of Congress Cataloging-in-Publication Data

Connolly, Kevin B.
      Buying and selling volatility / Kevin B. Connolly.
          p. cm.
      Includes index.
      ISBN 0-471-96884-6
      1. OPtions (Finance)   I. Title.
      HG6024.A3C66   1997
      332.63´228-dc21   96–46655
                                                          CIP

British Library Cataloguing in Publication Data

A catalogue record for this book is available from the British Library

ISBN 0-471-96884-6

Typeset in 11/13pt Times from the author's disks by
Footnote Graphics, Warminster, Wiltshire
Printed and bound in Great Britain by Biddles Ltd, Guildford and King's Lynn
This book is printed on acid-free paper responsibly manufactured from sustainable forestation,
for which at least two trees are planted for each one used for paper production.

Contents

Glossary of Terms

American Style Option an option can be exercised at any time prior to expiry.

At-the-money Option an option whose exercise price is at or very near the price of the underlying.

Call Option an option that gives the holder the right, but not the obligation, to buy the underlying from the call writer at a fixed price. This right expires on the expiry date. In the context of this book the underlying is stock or equity.

Call Spread (Vertical) a portfolio consisting of a long position in one call option and a short position in another call option. The options have different exercise prices but the same expiry.

Delta the rate of change of an option price with respect to a change in the underlying. The delta is a measure of the sensitivity of the option price to changes in the price of the underlying. Also known as the hedge ratio.

Delta Contour a line or curve on the standard price series chart connecting all points with the same delta. The delta contour gives an indication of how the sensitivity of an option changes over time as the underlying price changes.

Dynamic Replication a process by which any option can be replicated. The process involves the continual buying or selling of the underlying in such a way that the net payoff is identical to the payoff of the desired option. The cost of options replicated dynamically will be a function of the volatility actually experienced. The cost of static exchange traded options is a function of future expected volatility.

European Style Option   one that can only be exercised on the final (expiry) day.

Exercise Price   the price at which the underlying is bought or sold when an option is exercised.

Exercise   for a call option, exercising is the act of turning an option to buy into actually buying the underlying. For a put option, exercising is the act of turning an option to sell into actually selling the underlying.

Expected Value   the long run probabilistic value of an uncertain outcome.

Expiry Date   the final day in the life of an option.

Exposure   the equivalent quantity of the underlying that gives exactly the same absolute profit or loss when the price change is small.

Fair Value or Price   an option is fairly priced if, in the long run, the profit to a given strategy is zero.

Floating volatility   when the volatility profile (smile or smirk) moves or floats up or down with the underlying price.

Gamma   the rate of change of the delta.

Hedge Ratio   *see* delta.

Hedging   the process of removing the risk of experiencing a profit or loss from an options position.

Historic Volatility   a measure of the volatility experienced over some previous period.

Implied Volatility   the volatility implied by the price of an option.

In-the-money Option   an in-the-money call option has an exercise price lower than the current price of the underlying. An in-the-money put option has an exercise price higher than the current price of the underlying.

Intrinsic Value   the value of an option if it were immediately exercised.

Linear Relationship   one that can be represented graphically by straight lines or planes.

Long Position buying a stock or an option results in what is known as a long position. Being long of something will produce a profit (loss) if the price increases (decreases).

Long Volatility a long volatility position is one that is long options (puts or calls) but at the same time is market neutral.

Maturity Date *see* expiry.

Non-linear Relationship one that, when represented graphically, involves curves not straight lines.

Out-of-the-money Option an out-of-the-money call option has an exercise price higher than the current price of the underlying. An out-of-the-money put option has an exercise price lower than the current price of the underlying.

Put Option an option that gives the holder the right, but not the obligation, to sell the underlying to the put writer at a fixed price. This right expires on the expiry date.

Put Spread a portfolio consisting of a long position in one put option and a short position in another put option.

Rehedging the process or rebalancing the market exposure of a portfolio of options.

Short Position selling a stock or an option as an opening trade results in what is known as a short position. Being short of something will produce a loss (profit) if the price increases (decreases).

Short Volatility a short volatility position is one that is short options (puts or calls) but at the same time is market neutral.

Simulation in the context of this book a simulation is the computer generation of an artificial stock price series and/or an option price series.

Stock Borrowing the process by which most individuals establish short stock positions.

Strike Price also known as exercise price.

Synthetic Options a synthetic option is generated by dynamically buying and selling stock. *See* dynamic replication.

Theta the rate of change of an option or portfolio of options with respect to time.

Time Decay *see* theta.

Time Spread a portfolio consisting of a long position in one option and a short position in another option. The options usually have the same exercise prices but different times to expiry.

Time Value the time value of an option is the difference between the option price and the intrinsic value.

Underlying the financial asset that underlies an option. In this book the underlying is always stock.

Vega the rate of change of an option or portfolio of options with respect to changes in volatility.

Volatility a measure of the degree of the fluctuations in the price of something.

Volatility Smile a special situation in which options with different strike prices have different implied volatilities. With a smile, the at-the-money strike has the lowest implied volatility and those either side increase with increasing distance.

Volatility Smirk a special situation in which options with different strike prices have different implied volatilities. With a smirk the implied volatility distribution is asymmetric. One type of smirk has lower strike prices with low volatilities and higher strike prices with higher volatilities. The reverse situation is also possible.

1
An Introduction to the Concept of Volatility Trading

1.1 TRADITIONAL INVESTMENT AND VIEW TAKING

To make a profit, most individual investors and fund managers are forced to take a view on the direction of the price of something. The traditional or fundamental strategy is to study all the aspects of the market-place, all the factors affecting the price or that might affect the price, the general state of the economy (if relevant) and decide on the value of the investment vehicle under study. In addition to the fundamentals, many also consider what are known as the technical factors. Technical analytic methods use the sequence of previous prices to come up with an investment recommendation. Using charts to discover particular price patterns (hopefully repeatable) or to high-light trends is a very common technical tool. Today, chartism has such widespread use that most investment institutions will employ one if not more chartists and their language and terms are in common use in the financial press.

When the average person in the street hears the term "investment", they usually think of stock or equity. Traditionally, most private individuals and fund managers restricted their attention to investing in the stock market and usually in their own domestic stock market at that. Also, many investors would (or could) only really attempt to capitalise on the price of a particular stock rising. If all the analysis showed that a given stock was undervalued or cheap and that the rest of the world had not yet discovered this (but were about to) then one bought and established what is known as a long position. If the decision was right then the stock price would rise and at a suitable point one sold, realising a profit. However, if all the analysis indicated that a particular stock was overvalued or expensive and that it was very likely that the price would fall significantly in the future, then most private investors would (or could) do nothing. With the exception of the USA, most private investors could not capitalise on falling stock prices. You had to own stock to sell it. You could not establish a short position (explained later). So until relatively recently, investment decisions were often restricted to domestic stocks and usually one had to buy first and sell later.

All this was changed by the development and growth of the derivative product industry. The private individual now has access to a much wider spectrum of prospective investments via exchange traded derivatives. Rather than just considering individual domestic stocks, it is now possible to take a view not only on the level of the domestic stock index, but on almost every major foreign stock index. In addition, derivatives trade on an enormous number of commodities including energy, metals, grains and meats. And now it is possible to speculate on the movements of many of the world currencies. But by far the largest growth has occurred in the interest rate derivative market. Before 1970, if one took the view that this or that government would increase or decrease interest rates, there was no vehicle with which either the individual could speculate or the fund manager hedge. Today, it is possible to take positions in short, medium or long-dated interest rate derivatives in the US, European and Japanese markets.

Of course, one of the main advantages of derivatives is that it is just as easy to take a negative (bearish) view as it is to take a positive (bullish) view. Derivatives allow everyone to attempt to capitalise on prices falling without owning the underlying entity. It is just as easy to sell at a high price first and buy at a low price later as to do it the other way round, the usual way, of buying first and selling second.

The growth in the information technology industry has led to the general availability of more and more information to the fundamental analyst. Developments in the personal computer industry have meant that extremely sophisticated technical analysis software is now available for the cost of a few hundred dollars. And access to exchange traded derivative markets has meant that almost anyone anywhere can take a bullish or bearish position in almost anything that has a price. However, whether following fundamental analysis or technical analysis or a combination of both, the ultimate investment decision is that one has to **buy or sell** something. The traditional investor has to take a **view** on the direction of the price. If one is right, a profit is enjoyed, if not a loss is suffered.

Between entering and exiting the trade many things can and often do happen. The price of the instrument may rise or fall. The price may begin to fluctuate violently or become moribund. The price may collapse 50%, stay at this depressed level for several months only then to rise in an orderly fashion and to settle back to the original entry price. The investor may make or lose money or possibly break even, but every day the position would be valued according to the latest market price. The value of the investment will vary from day to day to a greater or lesser extent depending on market conditions. Most market participants refer to this variability as volatility and volatility to most traditional view-taking investors is not considered to be a good thing. Widely fluctuating prices can cause concern. Increasing volatility usually means there is increasing uncertainty in the market about the ultimate direction of the price.

The interesting point about the position of view-taking investors is that they are really only concerned with two prices—their entry and their exit price. So in a given year of say 240 trading days, if the investor gets into a position on day 60 and leaves on day 180, these two prices are all that are important. What happens between the getting in and the getting out in a way is irrelevant. Between entry and exit, the market may have been extremely volatile or very quiet. The view taker, once in, is just looking for an exit point. The view taker, in a sense, is looking at **only one dimension** of a price sequence—the direction. The view taker needs to get the direction of this dimension correct. Some view takers are spectacularly successful and seem to get the direction right more times than wrong. But many view takers only manage to get it right 50% of the time and many consistently fail. Most investors will agree that it is very difficult, even using the most sophisticated techniques, to consistently pick price trends correctly.

The purpose of this book is to show that there is **another dimension** to investment—trading the volatility of a price and not the direction. In the simple example above, of the investor entering a trade on day 60 and leaving on day 180, it is possible to devise strategies that will exploit any volatility that occurs between the two days. More importantly, it is possible to devise strategies that, under certain circumstances, will yield a profit without the need to take a view on the direction of the price at all. These techniques that trade the second dimension are known as volatility trades and the real attraction of them is that one can completely ignore the first dimension.

Imagine entering into a position in a given stock and not caring whether the price goes up or down. This is the very position of the volatility trader.

1.2   THREE EXAMPLES OF BUYING VOLATILITY

Before we go into the details of the more complex aspects of buying and selling volatility it is instructive first to consider some simple examples. These examples are simulations specifically chosen to highlight the irrelevance of view taking in this strategy. In each example we consider a different path a particular stock takes over the course of a year. For simplicity the year is split up into 52 weekly periods. The stock price and the profit or loss to the strategy are recorded each week and plotted in Figures 1.1 to 1.3. In all three examples the stock price at the start of the year is set to 1,000 units (dollars, pounds, yen or whatever). To illustrate the point that the profit or loss is independent of direction, the three examples depict situations in which (i) the stock price rises over the course of the year, (ii) the stock price falls over the course of the year and (iii) the stock price ends up unchanged.

How are the Stock Price Sequences Generated?

It is not really necessary to go into the details of how these sets of stock prices were generated. There are many different methods of price simulation and probably the simplest is to toss a coin. If the result is a head then increase the price by a given percentage (say 0.5%). If the result is a tail then decrease the price by the same amount. A method similar to but more complex than this, was used to generate the three sets of simulations. The method used ensured that each price change was independent of the previous price change. In this way the prices have "no memory", or exhibit no particular pattern.

Is This Really Realistic and Does it Have Implications for the Profit and Loss of the Strategy?

Some chartists would probably disagree with the simulations and say that these do not represent a real life stock price process. Chartists believe that prices are non-random. However, the important point to note is that although these three examples are generated by **random processes** the strategy is equally valid if the processes were non-random and had some hidden pattern. A random process is used just to illustrate a point.

The Outcomes of the Three Strategies

The long volatility strategy is a simple set of trading rules that dictate the buying or selling of either the stock or a derivative instrument related to the stock. Trading only occurs when certain criteria are met. At no time is a view taken on the stock price direction and at no time are forecasts of the future stock price required. Most importantly, exactly the same trading rule is used in all three examples.

Example 1

In Figure 1.1 the stock price starts at 1,000 and over the course of the year gradually rises to 1,300. The stock price increase is not in a perfect straight line. There are fluctuations. The price does move up and down, i.e. there is some volatility. In this example the up moves eventually dominated the down moves resulting in a price rise of 300 points or 30% by the end of the year. The long volatility strategy profit (shown by the dotted line) over the same period and using the

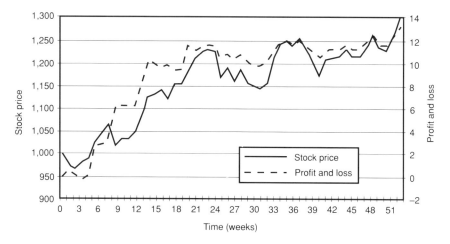

Figure 1.1   Long volatility simulation no. 1

same scale was 13 points. With hindsight, of course, it would have been better to simply have bought the stock and enjoyed a profit of 300 points. But consider the risk. If the stock price had fallen, a loss maybe as high as 300 points would have occurred.

In this example because both the stock price and the profit increase together it may appear that the two are correlated. This is not so. The stock price rises are due to chance and the profits are due to stock price volatility.

Example 2

In Figure 1.2 the stock price starts at 1,000 and over the course of the year gradually falls to 750. Again the fall is not in a perfect straight line. There are fluctuations. The prices move up and down and there is also some volatility. In this example the down moves eventually dominated the up moves resulting in a price drop of 250 points or 25% by the end of the year. The long volatility strategy profit over the same period and using the same scale was 13 points. With hindsight, of course, it would have been better to simply have shorted the stock and enjoyed a profit of 250 points. But consider the risk. If the stock price had risen significantly, a loss would have occurred.

In this example, because the stock price and the profit move in opposite directions it may appear that the two are negatively correlated. This is not so.

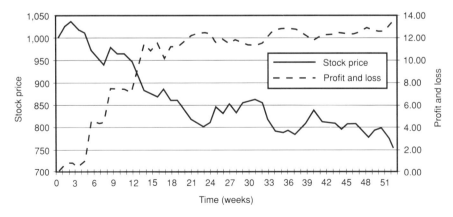

Figure 1.2   Long volatility simulation no. 2

Example 3

In Figure 1.3 the stock price starts at 1,000, falls initially and then rises to end up back at 1,000 by the year end. As in examples 1 and 2, the stock price exhibited some volatility throughout the year. A directional investor (long or short) would have broken even over the period. The long volatility player would have produced a profit of 34 points.

Why is the profit in this example over twice that in the previous two? There are two reasons. One is that the derivative used in these simulations has special properties if the stock price continues to move around the 1,000 level. The second is that the volatility of the stock in this example is slightly higher than in examples 1 and 2. Later we will explain these special characteristics and how to measure stock price volatility.

These three examples illustrate that using exactly the same trading strategy, a profit can be made irrespective of price direction. However, it should be pointed out that a profit does not always result. If the stock price exhibits little or no volatility then it is possible to experience a loss. In the jargon of the market "you have to pay for volatility" and if you experience none then there is a possibility of incurring a loss.

1.3 THE INSTRUMENTS

To buy or sell volatility involves constructing a portfolio of at least two instruments. In its simplest form, the portfolio will have positions (long or short) in the stock and a derivative of the stock. There are

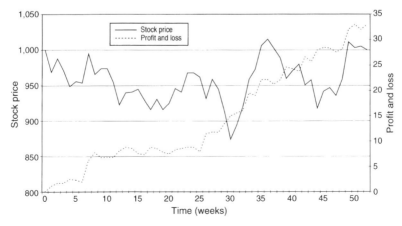

Figure 1.3   Long volatility simulation no. 3

many types of derivatives, and examples include: futures, call options, put options, warrants and convertible bonds. The volatility strategies require that the derivatives must have a curved price profile (explained later) and this limits the set to those having option type characteristics. Call options on stocks are intuitively easy to understand. Accordingly, to simplify the exposition even further, we restrict the discussion throughout most of the book to one considering portfolios of stock and stock call options.

Portfolios constructed to exploit volatility will always have opposing positions in stock and stock call options. The mix has to be balanced in such a way that the profit or loss on one component will always cancel the loss or profit on the other component. The total portfolio will thus be fully hedged and hence have no exposure to the market. This is why the volatility player need not take a view. The portfolio (initially anyway) is not exposed to risk associated with the stock price direction. Estimating the special ratio of components, deciding what to do when the stock price eventually moves and how to extract the volatility profit will be outlined in later chapters. Before we go into these complexities we need to define some standard investment terms.

───── 2 ─────
A Review
of Some Basic Concepts

In this chapter we take a fresh look at some of the standard terminology used in finance. Most readers will be familiar with expressions such as long, short, market exposure and profit and loss. The discussion in this book eventually leads on to certain non-mathematical aspects of option pricing and it is here that some non-standard terms are introduced. "A picture tells a thousand stories" and this is certainly very true of the more complex ideas associated with volatility trades. All of the above terminology and most of the more complex ideas will be explained graphically. We will show that to get a real understanding of volatility trading is all about understanding rates of change. The best way to understand the concept of **rates of change** is to look at pictures.

2.1 RATES OF CHANGE AND GRADIENTS OF STRAIGHT LINES

In this section we will be examining and measuring the relationship between sets of variables. The relationships will be artificial and will be depicted in three ways: (i) in a table form, (ii) graphically and (iii) using a rate of change measure. In each case we look at pairs of observations of two imaginary variables X and Y. In each case we imagine that X "drives" Y, i.e. that Y depends solely on X and that X depends on something external. We will be interested in measuring the relationship between Y and X and in particular the rate at which Y changes with respect to X. This will eventually lead on to real life

Table 2.1 Simple linear relationships

X	Y	Z
100	200	260
110	205	265
120	210	270
130	215	275
140	220	280
150	225	285

situations where X will be the price of a stock and Y the value of a portfolio containing the stock or stock derivative.

First consider Table 2.1 listing six sets of values of X and Y. It is obvious that the link between Y and X is perfect. As one considers the increasing values of X: 100, 110, 120, ... the values of Y also increase: 200, 205, 210, ... Each change in Y by 5 units is "caused" by a change of 10 units in X. Figure 2.1 depicts the situation graphically. Connecting the six points to form a straight line is a standard device to illustrate the link between the two variables. Mathematicians refer to relationships like this as **linear** for obvious reasons. The virtue of linear or straight-line-type relationships is that they can be characterised very easily by one simple number: the gradient or slope of the line. Draw any right-angled triangle under the straight line and the gradient is simply the ratio of the vertical side divided by the horizontal side. In Figure 2.1 using triangle ABC the ratio is 1 to 2. Gradients are typically expressed as ratios or percentages and so the gradient of this linear relationship is

$$\text{Gradient} = \frac{25}{50} = 0.50 \quad (\text{or } 50\%)$$

Of course this answer was obvious from Table 2.1. As X increases by 10, Y increases by 5. If X were to increase by 5, Y would increase by 2.5. If X were to increase by 1, Y would increase by 0.5. In short, the rate of change of Y with respect to X is 0.5 or 50%.

Table 2.1 also lists the values of a third variable Z. As X increases from 100 to 110 to 120, etc., Z increases from 260 to 265 to 270, etc. The variable Z starts on a different level from Y but has exactly the same relationship to X, i.e. the rate of change is also 0.50. Graphically this is equivalent to having parallel lines. In Figure 2.1 we see that the gradients of both lines are indeed identical at 0.50. The responsiveness

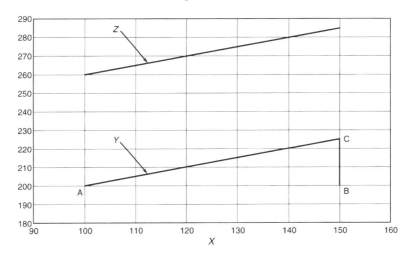

Figure 2.1 Simple linear relationships

of both variables to changes in X is identical. It is important in what follows to understand that the actual value or level of a variable such as Y or Z is often irrelevant; it is the rate of change of the value with respect to X that matters.

Consider Table 2.2 that lists four imaginary linear relationships $Y(I)$, $Y(II)$, $Y(III)$ and $Y(IV)$. The corresponding graphical representation appears in Figure 2.2. The tabulated numbers and the straight lines of varying gradients both illustrate that the relationships have varying degrees of rates of change. Relationship (I) is similar to the one considered above, i.e. Y increases at 0.50 of the rate of X. With relationships (II), (III) and (IV) the rates of change are 0.30, 0.80 and 1.00 respectively. Higher rates of change are represented by steeper straight lines.

Table 2.2 Examples of different positive rates of change

X	$Y(I)$	$Y(II)$	$Y(III)$	$Y(IV)$
100	200	200	200	200
110	205	203	208	210
120	210	206	216	220
130	215	209	224	230
140	220	212	232	240
150	225	215	240	250

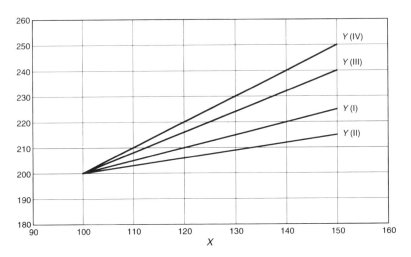

Figure 2.2 Linear relationships with different rates of change

Finally consider Table 2.3 and Figure 2.3. These examples illustrate situations in which, as X increases in steps of 10 units, Y decreases in steps of different amounts. The same principle applies to measuring the rate of change, except that if the direction of the change of Y is opposite to that of X we define the gradient and the rate of change as negative. So relationship (I) in which Y decreases 3 units as X increases 10 units is said to have a gradient or rate of change of -0.30. Graphically the procedure is the same except that the right-angled triangle is now drawn upside down and the length of the vertical side will have an associated minus sign. From Figure 2.3 we can calculate the gradient of the line (I) from the triangle ABC as

$$\text{Gradient} = \frac{-15}{50} = -0.30 \quad (\text{or } -30\%)$$

Table 2.3 Examples of different negative rates of change

X	Y(I)	Y(II)	Y(III)	Y(IV)
100	200	200	200	200
110	197	195	192	190
120	194	190	184	180
130	191	185	176	170
140	188	180	168	160
150	185	175	160	150

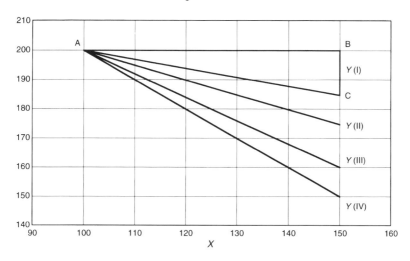

Figure 2.3   Linear relationships with negative rates of change

Note that the magnitude of the gradient still defines the steepness. Line (IV) has a gradient of −1 or −100% and describes the relationship with the maximum rate of change albeit in the reverse sense.

2.2   LONG AND SHORT

Although these terms have already been mentioned it is useful to expand on the definition of a long or short position. The most straightforward position is to be long. A long position is one that will be profitable if the price of something rises. Most individuals have a concept of being long—you simply buy something and hope the price rises and then sell. The profit will be the difference between the purchase and sale price. If, of course, the price falls you suffer a negative profit, i.e. a loss. It is easy to think of buying a stock or a given quantity of a commodity or even a given number of foreign currency units. Probably more abstract is the concept of going long a futures contract. However, the principle is the same. When you buy a futures contract you enter into an agreement that commits you to a long position. It does not really matter what is underlying the futures contract. All that matters is that you want the price to rise so that you can sell at a profit.

Initially, to the inexperienced, the concept of entering a short position can be confusing. In the jargon of the market-place one "sells short". But how can you sell something you do not own? If we forget this issue for the moment and just say that entering a short position will result in a profit if the price falls and a loss if the price rises. With futures contracts, shorting is quite straightforward if one forgets about the underlying financial instrument. Opening a short position is simply entering into a contract that guarantees a profit if the price falls and guarantees a loss if the price rises. A short position is closed out with a buy transaction. If the opening (selling) price is higher than the closing (buying) price then a profit results. One will have bought something low and sold high but in a back to front sense. Provided the purchase price is lower than the sale price, a profit will result. The fact that the transactions are carried out in the reverse time order to what one is usually accustomed to, is really irrelevant since nothing ever changes hands only contracts defining commitments.

Shorting something real like stock can be more complex. Typically one uses a technique known as **borrowing**. As an illustration consider the following example. A certain stock is trading in the market at $100 and an individual believes that in the near future the price will fall significantly. The individual whom we shall refer to as the shorter or Mr S, knows a fund manager, Mr FM, who has a large position in the stock and this position is likely to remain unchanged even if his prediction of a price fall proves true. Mr S approaches Mr FM and asks to borrow the stock for a certain period of time. Mr FM agrees in return for a deposit equal to the price of the stock, i.e. $100. Mr S deposits $100 cash with Mr FM and physically receives the stock which he then sells on into the market-place. Mr S has sold the borrowed stock and so has received $100 cash from the buyer. The situation is now as follows.

- **Mr S:** Mr S has placed a deposit of $100 cash with Mr FM, received $100 cash from the stock buyer and so is cash neutral. He has, however, a commitment to Mr FM to return the stock to him on or before some time in the future. Since Mr S has no stock as such, he is essentially short. At some point in the future he will have to get (i.e. buy) the stock from the market to deliver to Mr FM.
- **Mr FM:** Mr FM has a deposit of $100 cash sitting on deposit earning interest. He still is long of the stock since he has not actually sold any but just lent some to Mr S. So Mr FM is still long (via a contract with Mr S) and has the advantage of receiving additional income for his funds.

In practice the interest earned from the cash deposit is split between Mr FM and Mr S under what is known as a repo agreement. We continue with this example and see what the outcome will be under the following two scenarios.

- **Scenario 1.** The stock price falls to $80. Mr S goes into the market and buys at $80 and delivers stock to Mr FM. Mr FM returns the deposit of $100 and the transaction is over. Mr FM still is long of the stock and has enjoyed additional income (or a fraction thereof). Mr S has bought the stock at $80 and sold at $100 realising a profit of $20.
- **Scenario 2.** The stock price rises to $120. Mr S goes into the market and buys at $120 and delivers stock to Mr FM. Mr FM returns the deposit of $100 and the transaction is over. Mr FM still is long of the stock and has enjoyed additional income (or a fraction thereof). Mr S has bought the stock at $120 and sold at $100 realising a loss of $20.

This all sounds very complicated but for most of the developed stock markets (excluding the UK) the process of stock borrowing is a very efficient business. Many participants, small and large, find it just as easy to go short as to go long.

2.3   PROFIT, LOSS AND PRICE CHANGES

Everyone understands what it means to experience a profit or loss. Often profits and losses are talked of in terms of percentage changes. In the world of derivative investments this is what leads to much confusion. It is much more straightforward to think in terms of the absolute change in the value of an investment rather than the percentage change. It is also considerably easier to represent profits or losses graphically if one uses an absolute measure. Accordingly throughout most of this book, profits and losses will be reported in terms of absolute changes, not percentage changes.

The investment community is used to studying charts of stock prices over time like the one in Figure 2.4. These are known as time series charts. In these types of diagrams the horizontal axis is always time and the vertical axis is always a price. By buying at A and selling at B or by shorting at C and buying back at D, a profit is realised. To understand the volatility trade it is more instructive to look at a different representation of profit and loss as in Figures 2.5–2.7.

Figure 2.5 shows the value of a portfolio of one share of stock versus the price of the stock and as such is, of course, extremely simple. Figure

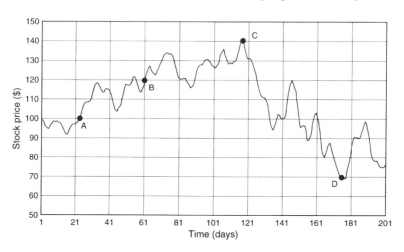

Figure 2.4   Time series chart of stock price

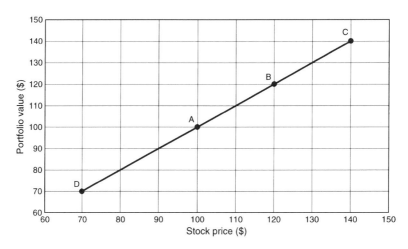

Figure 2.5   Value of portfolio of one share

2.6 gives the change in the value of a portfolio of one share assuming the share was purchased at point A, i.e. at a price of $100. This chart represents the profit or loss (in absolute terms) on a long position in one share. In both these charts the horizontal axis is the price of the

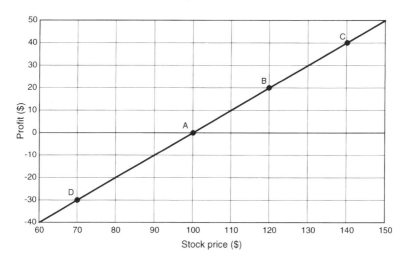

Figure 2.6 Profit profile of *long* position in one share

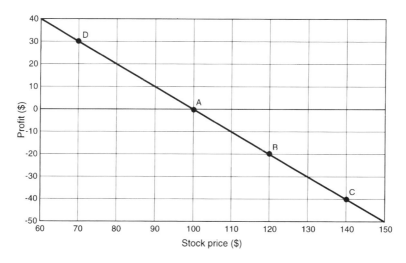

Figure 2.7 Profit of *short* position in one share

share and not time. As a result, the time sequence of the points A, B, C and D is lost. Note also that the gradient of the lines are 1 or 100%. These may seem like very obvious statements to make but it will become crucial later on to realise the importance of this apparently simple way of looking at profits and losses in terms of slopes of straight lines. Figure 2.7 gives the profit and loss to a short position in one share and obviously has a gradient of -1 or -100%.

2.4 THE IMPORTANCE OF USING EXPOSURE AND NOT COST TO MEASURE RISK

Profit and loss charts such as Figures 2.6 and 2.7 also give the **stock exposure**. The gradient of the profit profiles defines the stock exposure. In Figure 2.6 the gradient is indicating that the investor is exposed to one share. The profit profile is perfectly linear and so the gradient is constant at all levels of stock price. When you are long of one share, your stock exposure is always one share, whatever the stock price. In Figure 2.7 the gradient is a constant -1 at all stock price levels. When you are short of one share, your stock exposure is always the reverse of being long one share, whatever the stock price.

Table 2.4 shows the value of three portfolios A, B and C over a range of different stock prices. Three fund managers were each given $1,000 and told that they could only invest in a specific stock (priced today at $100) and/or cash. They could keep some or all of the cash on deposit or borrow up to a maximum of $500 for further investment. To make the numbers simple we will assume that they receive no

Table 2.4 Stock plus cash portfolios

Stock price	Value of Portfolio A 10 units of stock	Value of Portfolio B 5 units of stock + $500 cash	Value of Portfolio C 15 units of stock − $500 cash
50	500	750	250
60	600	800	400
70	700	850	550
80	800	900	700
90	900	950	850
100	1,000	1,000	1,000
110	1,100	1,050	1,150
120	1,200	1,100	1,300
130	1,300	1,150	1,450
140	1,400	1,200	1,600
150	1,500	1,250	1,750

interest on deposits and that borrowing costs are zero. The manager of portfolio A buys 10 shares at $100, spending the full $10 \times 100 = $1,000 and is thus 100% invested in the stock. The manager of portfolio B decides to be more cautious, buys five shares, spending $5 \times 100 = $500 and keeps the remaining $500 on deposit. The manager of portfolio C is much more aggressive on the future of the stock price and so borrows $500, which together with the original $1,000 enables this manager to buy 15 shares.

Table 2.5 and Figure 2.8 show the profit or loss on the portfolios. The figures are obtained by subtracting the initial investment value of $1,000 from the corresponding portfolio values in Table 2.4. The gradient of the profit profiles of A, B and C are 10, 5 and 15 respectively. These gradients give the correct exposure to the risk associated with the stock. The market price (or cost) of the portfolios does not enter into consideration. If the three funds were priced at the time of inception, all would have the same value of $1,000. A common mistake, especially in the derivative market, is that if one buys something for $1,000 then the tendency is to think that this is all the risk one is exposed to. This is most definitely not the case. An investor buying into fund A, B or C will be exposed to completely different risks. The price is irrelevant. It is the rate of change of the price that is important. One needs to be able to estimate by how much the invest-

Table 2.5 Profit and loss of portfolios A, B and C

Stock price	Value of Portfolio A 10 units of stock	Value of Portfolio B 5 units of stock + $500 cash	Value of Portfolio C 15 units of stock − $500 cash
50	−500	−250	−750
60	−400	−200	−600
70	−300	−150	−450
80	−200	−100	−300
90	−100	−50	−150
100	0	0	0
110	+100	+50	+150
120	+200	+100	+300
130	+300	+150	+450
140	+400	+200	+600
150	+500	+250	+750
Rate of change	+10	+5	+15

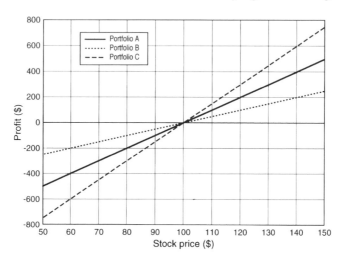

Figure 2.8 Stock plus cash portfolios

ment will move if the underlying stock price moves. One needs to be able to estimate the rate of change or the gradient of the profit profile.

2.5 A NONLINEAR PROFIT PROFILE OF AN IMAGINARY INVESTMENT

The gradients of the profit and loss profiles of portfolios A, B and C above are constant throughout the entire range of stock prices. The stock exposure of each portfolio was thus fixed at all price levels. This is not usually the case with portfolios involving derivatives and in fact is deliberately designed not to be so with volatility trades. Before we proceed, it is instructive to consider what the profit and loss changes one would experience by investing in an instrument that had variable stock exposure.

As an example, consider investing in an imaginary "black box" portfolio. The contents of the black box portfolio are unknown. All one is told is that the value of the portfolio varies as a certain stock price varies. The relationship between the portfolio value and the stock price is given in Table 2.6 and Figure 2.9.

- **Region P to N.** We consider the situation on a day when the stock price is at a $100 and the portfolio is valued at $40,000. We buy into the portfolio or go long at $40,000. We are at point M in Figure 2.9. Immediately after the purchase, the price of the stock begins to move about. First up $10 to $110, then down $20 to $90. Notice that the black box portfolio also changes in value. With the stock price up $10 the portfolio increases in value by $10,000. With a fall of $20 the value falls $20,000. It "feels" as if the portfolio is just long of 1,000 shares, i.e. the stock exposure is 1,000 shares. Notice that the portfolio actually only costs $40,000. To generate the same sort of stock exposure one would normally have to pay 1,000 × 100 = $100,000. Around point M, although we only invested $40,000 it is as if we are invested in $100,000 worth of shares. This is entirely feasible. Just consider the simple situation in section 2.4 in which the fund manager borrowed funds to leverage up exposure.

- **Region N to L.** Let us assume that the stock price now rises above $130, i.e. above point N. Between N and L the slope of the value line halves to 500. We are not told what is happening inside the portfolio, just that further $10 up moves in the stock price only produce additional profits of $5,000. Suddenly we are in the situation of only being exposed to half the amount of stock we were previously exposed to. It is as if the black box

Table 2.6   Imaginary black box portfolio

Point	Stock price ($)	Portfolio value ($)	Change in Portfolio value ($)
R	0	60,000	−10,000
	10	50,000	−10,000
	20	40,000	−10,000
	30	30,000	−10,000
Q	40	20,000	0
	50	20,000	0
	60	20,000	0
	70	20,000	0
P	80	20,000	+10,000
	90	30,000	+10,000
M	**100**	**40,000**	**+10,000**
	110	50,000	+10,000
	120	60,000	+10,000
N	130	70,000	+5,000
	140	75,000	+5,000
	150	80,000	+5,000
	160	85,000	+5,000
L	170	90,000	+20,000
	180	110,000	+20,000
	190	130,000	+20,000
	200	150,000	—

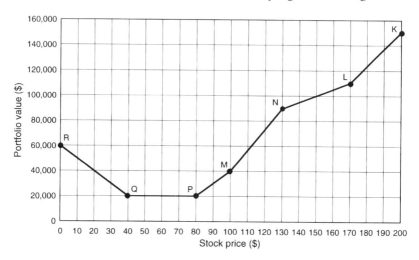

Figure 2.9 Black box portfolio value

fund manager sold half the stock at point N. Between N and L the stock exposure is 500 units.

- **Region L to K.**   If the stock price continues to rise above the point L we get into another situation. Now for every $10 rise the portfolio value increases by $20,000. The slope of the line and hence the stock exposure are now 2,000.
- **Region P to Q.**   Now consider the situation if the stock price falls all the way to a point below $80 but above $40, i.e. between P and Q. Between these two points the portfolio value is constant at $20,000 and does not depend on the stock price at all. The slope of the line and hence the stock exposure are zero. It is as if the fund manager has sold out the entire inventory leaving just a cash sum of $20,000.
- **Region Q to R.**   Below $40 (point Q) we have the reverse situation in that as the price falls $10 the portfolio value increases by $10,000. The slope of the line QR is −1,000. Clearly the stock exposure here is negative, or short 1,000 shares.

The purpose of this imaginary example is to emphasise that the stock exposure of an investment need not have anything to do with the price of the investment and that the exposure need not be constant or linear. It is all about the sensitivity of the investment to a stock price move. This sensitivity or stock exposure is measured by the slope of the price of the investment, not the actual level or value of the investment. With volatility trades we specifically design portfolios in such a way that the exposure varies constantly with the underlying share price.

2.6 A REAL LIFE EXAMPLE OF A NONLINEAR PRICE PROFILE

The black box portfolio in section 2.5 is very contrived and was used just to illustrate a point. There are, however, real instruments that exhibit some of the same nonlinear type properties. One such example is a **convertible bond** (CB). CBs are issued by corporations as a way of raising capital. The simplest type of CB pays a fixed coupon per year and can either be redeemed like a straight bond or **converted** into shares. The holder of the CB has to choose whether to redeem into cash or convert into shares. No additional payments are required with either option. CBs have a fixed maturity date, so the holder eventually has to decide—cash or shares? Consider the following simple example.

A CB, convertible into one share of stock, is about to mature. The redemption value of the CB is $100 and there are no further coupons due.

- **Share Price at $110.** What is the CB worth if the share price on maturity is $110? Obviously the holder would elect to take the shares and immediately sell these into the market and recoup $110. It would not make sense to redeem for the fixed cash sum of $100.
- **Share Price at $120.** What is the CB worth if the share price on maturity is $120? Obviously the holder would elect to take the shares and immediately sell these into the market and recoup $120. In fact at any price above $100 it would always make sense to convert into shares.
- **Share Price at $90.** What is the CB worth if the share price on maturity is $90? In this case converting into shares would not make sense. It would be better to take the cash sum of $100. In fact at any price below $100 it would always make sense to take the cash option.

Table 2.7 and Figure 2.10 give the value of the CB on the maturity date for various stock price levels. The price profile is clearly nonlinear. At stock prices above $100, the slope of the profile is one—the instrument behaves exactly like one unit of stock. At stock prices below $100, the slope is zero—the instrument is completely independent and behaves like cash pool of $100. This is the situation of all CBs on the maturity date. The nonlinearity, or kink at $100, is caused by the simple fact that the holder has the **option** to do one thing or another. The very fact that the holder can choose, **on maturity**, between having exposure to stock or cash has implications for the pricing of the instrument **before maturity**. It is the pricing of such an instrument before maturity that is more complex and we consider these aspects in more detail in Chapter 3.

Table 2.7   Value of convertible bond on
maturity

Stock price on maturity ($)	Convertible price on maturity ($)
50	100
60	100
70	100
80	100
90	100
100	100
110	110
120	120
130	130
140	140
150	150
160	160

2.7   MEASURING VOLATILITY

Everyone has a concept of volatility when used in connection with finance or investment. The stock market crash of October 1987 saw the Dow Jones Industrial Average Index fall 512 points (25%) in one day only to rebound 60 points the next day. This caused similar crashes and associated increases in price volatility around the world. Although most increases in market volatility are thought of as being associated with large price falls this is not always the case. The price of gold increased 200% in 1979 in a matter of only six months and the price of crude oil increased 160% in the three months leading up to the Gulf War in 1990. Stock markets are sent into panic by investors fleeing to liquidate into cash and commodities are often disrupted by market short squeezes. The ERM crises in Britain in September 1992 caused the short-term interest rate market to increase in volatility dramatically. Sterling rates went from 10 to 12 to 15% and back down to 10% and all in one day.

Although most individuals have a concept of what market volatility is, few know how it is measured and many confuse volatility with direction. This book is devoted to explaining the concept of being able to buy or sell volatility and so it is important to be able to understand how it is measured. When setting up a long or short volatility position

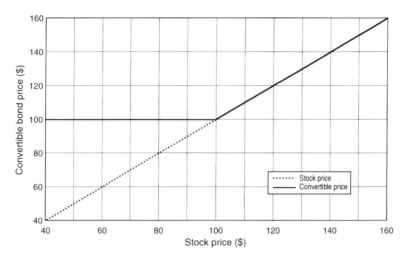

Figure 2.10 Convertible bond price on maturity

it is important to have an idea of what future volatility one is expecting and what this really means in terms of price changes.

The strict definition of volatility as used by market participants is quite complex and involves the use of natural logarithms and a knowledge of the statistics associated with what is known as the **lognormal distribution**. However, it is possible to understand volatility measurements using far simpler ideas and this is the approach we use here. Although the following examples are very simple it should be noted that these are just for exposition purposes only and the exact definition of volatility, if required, is given in most textbooks on option pricing. It should also be noted that many market participants never have to go to the bother of actually calculating the volatility of a price series. Most of the information services such as Bloomberg and Reuters provide estimates of historic volatility and many provide excellent charts showing how the volatility of a given series has changed over time. In addition to estimates of historic volatility these services also provide information on what is known as the **implied volatility**. The implied volatility is probably one of the most important measures for the volatility player and will be dealt with later.

The term "volatility of a price series" is really a misnomer. When practitioners talk of volatility of a price series they are actually referring to the volatility of a series of **price changes** or relative price changes. As with the concept of stock exposure, it is important to realise that the price of the stock under consideration is completely irrelevant; it is the change in the price that matters. As with many concepts in investment, it is not the price level that is important, it is the way the price is changing. We can think of a series of price changes as being "caused" by time passing. In measuring volatility we are interested in the way in which the passing of time affects the price changes.

A complication associated with looking at a series of prices and price changes is accounting for the presence of trend. Volatility is supposed to measure the degree of fluctuations, not the trend. If there is a trend then we need to look at the fluctuations around the trend. If the stock price is higher (lower) at the end of a period than at the beginning we say that there is positive (negative) trend. This point is illustrated in the following specially contrived examples given in Figure 2.11. The numbers are chosen so that the series have identical trend. Price series (I) starts on day one at $100 and increases uniformly at $1 a day for 10 days. Price series (II) also starts on day one at $100 but increases in a non-uniform manner. Both series end up at the same price of $110 and so have the same trend of on average +$1 a day. The second panel in Figure 2.11 shows the respective daily price changes. It is clear that series (II) exhibits volatility and that series (I) does not. The changes in series (I) are all $1 whereas those of series (II) vary. The average change or trend for both series is $1 a day but with series (II) there is some variation around this average. And that leads us on to a definition of volatility.

The volatility of a price series is a measure of the deviation of price changes around the trend.

Although this sounds complex it is really quite easy to calculate. The details of the calculations for series (II) are given in Table 2.8.

Column (c) in Table 2.8 gives the deviations of the changes around the average trend. The volatility measure we are looking for is one number summing up the magnitude of all of these deviations. If these deviations are large we say that the series is very volatile, and if they are small we say the series is not very volatile. We need one descriptive statistic that will summarise the overall magnitude of the deviations and the most obvious one would be the average. However, by definition some of these deviations are positive and some are negative, and it is easy to prove that they will always cancel out and

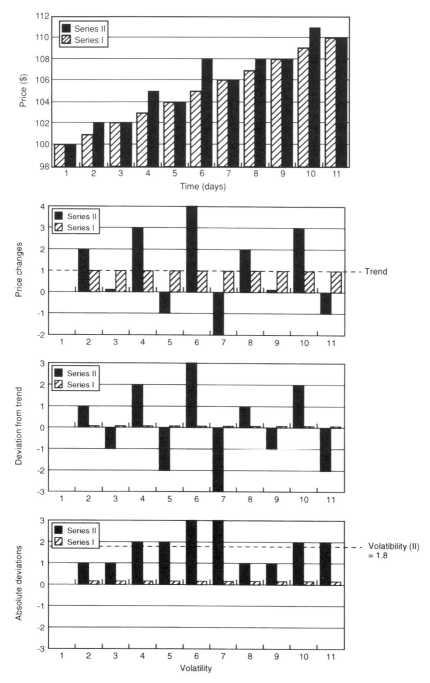

Figure 2.11 Calculation of volatility

that the total and hence the average will always be zero. So one cannot use the average. An easy solution is obtained if we note that we are really only interested in the magnitude of the deviations and not their sign. We know that all the positive deviations will always equal the negative deviations so let us just consider the absolute value of the deviations and these are given in column (d). The average of this column is 1.8 and we interpret this as the average deviation about the trend value. This then is the volatility of the series. Series II is a sequence of prices that has an average trend of $1 a day with volatility around this trend of $1.8 a day. It is left as an exercise for the reader to prove that series I has zero volatility.

Figure 2.12 shows three simulated price series with different degrees of volatility and trend. In these series the volatilities are given in terms of $s per week. The most volatile series has a mean absolute deviation (volatility) of $4 per week. One could express this volatility as a percentage of the original stock price and say that the volatility is 4% on a weekly basis. Thus we could compare two stocks, one trading at $100 and another trading at $200. If they both have the same percentage volatility then the second stock would on average fluctuate $8 around the mean trend.

The strict definition of volatility as used by market participants uses a function of relative price changes rather than price changes and the

Table 2.8 The calculation of a volatility measure for series II

Day	Stock price ($)	Price change (a)	Average price change (trend) (b)	Deviation (c) = (a) − (b)	Absolute deviation (d) = |(c)|
1	100	—	—	—	—
2	102	+2	+1	+1	+1
3	102	0	+1	−1	+1
4	105	+3	+1	+2	+2
5	104	−1	+1	−2	+2
6	108	+4	+1	+3	+3
7	106	−2	+1	−3	+3
8	108	+2	+1	+1	+1
9	108	0	+1	−1	+1
10	111	+3	+1	+2	+2
11	110	−1	+1	−2	+2
Total	—	**+10**			**+18**
Average	—	**+10/10 = +1**			**+18/10 = 1.8**

results are always given in annual terms even if the period under consideration is only three months. Typical volatility values might be say 20% for an individual stock, 13% for a stock index and 40% for a highly volatile commodity. The exact interpretation of the absolute deviation volatility measure used in the examples above is straightforward but that of the standard one used in the market is more complex. However, both measure the same property: the degree of price deviation around some mean trend. One use of the standard volatility measure is to make probability statements about the approximate likely range of the stock price in the future. Assuming that the standard volatility of a series is x%, then in one year's time:

1. There is a 66% chance that the stock price is in the range (100 − x)% to (100 + x)% of the price today.
2. There is a 95% chance that the stock price is in the range (100 − $2x$)% to (100 + $2x$)% of the price today.
3. There is a 99% chance that the stock price is in the range (100 − $3x$)% to (100 + $3x$)% of the price today.

So if the stock price today is $200 and the volatility of a stock is 25% then there is a 66% chance of the stock price being in the range $150 to $250. These statements are only approximate but give one an idea of the likely spread of future prices.

There are a number of sampling type problems associated with the

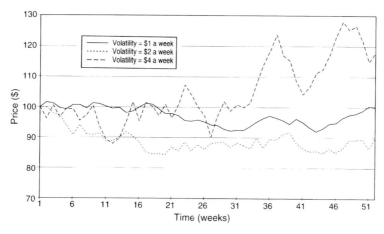

Figure 2.12 Simulated price series

estimation of volatility. Do we use daily, weekly or monthly prices? Also how far back in time do we go? The accuracy of all statistics is a direct function of the sample size. Using 200 sample points is better than using 50. So in calculating the volatility of the price of IBM stock do we go back 200 weeks or 50 weeks? If we go back as far as 200 weeks we may be including data that are so out of date as to be increasing, rather than reducing, the error of the estimate. Empirical evidence suggests that volatility is constantly changing and so it is important not to go too far back in time. Another issue is that of using inter-day data. In the above we used one price per day and many practitioners are content with the results obtained from daily closing prices. Some traders advocate using more than one piece of information per day such as the open, high, low and close.

Unfortunately there is no one correct solution to the estimation of volatility. Like many other aspects of finance, whatever estimate one uses it is only historic and it should not be assumed that past volatility is a good forecast for future volatility. This does not mean that historic volatility estimates are not useful; it just means that one must be careful with the interpretation. There is evidence for what is known as "reversion to the mean" with volatility. Simply put, this means that if a particular price series begins to exhibit high volatility this will eventually fall. Similarly if the series begins to exhibit particularly low volatility then it will eventually rise. The theory suggests the presence of some long-term average volatility level. The trick is of course picking the high and low volatility points.

3
The Price Profile of Derivatives before Expiry

The convertible bond mentioned in Chapter 2 is just one example of a derivative instrument that has a kinked price profile on expiry. Convertible bonds are particularly easy to understand. The choice is between a lump sum of cash and the stock price. The decision is an easy one: take the option that is worth the most. The problem is that the price profile is kinked only on one day—the day of expiry. What does the price profile look like before expiry? Below we address this question by considering a much more widely known derivative instrument—the call option.

3.1 THE CALL OPTION

There are markets in call options on stocks, commodities, currencies, stock indexes, futures and interest rates. Each type of option is priced slightly differently but the general price behaviour of all call options can be understood by considering just one type: an option to call stock. Accordingly throughout this book we will always refer to stock call options.

Definition A stock call option gives the right but not the obligation to buy a given quantity of stock at a given price on or before a given date.

The given quantity is fixed and is usually either 100 units or 1,000 units. The given price is known as the **exercise price** or **strike price** and the given date is known as the **expiry date**. Often the stock underlying the option is simply referred to as **the underlying**.

As an example, IBM options give the right to buy 100 units of IBM stock. There will be many IBM options available and we consider just one. On a day when the stock price is, say, $102, there will be an option with an exercise price of $100 expiring in three months' time. We leave the issue of what the option costs for the moment and go straight to the expiry date three months hence. The holder of the option must decide what to do.

1. The holder can "exercise" the option and elect to buy stock at the exercise price of $100. In this case the exercise amount must be paid in full and in return the holder will receive 100 units of stock—the holder has **called** stock at $100, hence the term "call option". If the holder exercises, it is necessary to pay an additional $100 \times 100 = \$10,000$. If the price of the stock is greater than the exercise price of $100 in the market then this route is optimal. If the stock is trading at $104 then the holder could immediately sell all 100 units realising a value of $4 per share or a total of $100 \times 4 = \$400$. If the stock is trading at $108 then the final value would be $100 \times 8 = \$800$.
2. The holder can choose not to exercise the option. If the stock is trading at $94 in the market then it clearly does not make sense to exercise the right to buy at $100. If stock was wanted, it could be bought cheaper in the market. In this situation the holder would let the option expire. This route would be chosen if the stock price in the market were anything less than the exercise price of $100. In this situation the option would not have any final value at all and we say that the option expires worthless.

Table 3.1 gives the final value of the call option for various final stock prices. Figure 3.1 is a graphical representation of this final value.

Table 3.1 Value of option with exercise price = $100 on expiry

Stock price on expiry ($)	Value of option ($) on expiry
90	0
92	0
94	0
96	0
98	0
100	0
102	$2 \times 100 = 200$
104	$4 \times 100 = 400$
106	$6 \times 100 = 600$
108	$8 \times 100 = 800$
110	$10 \times 100 = 1000$

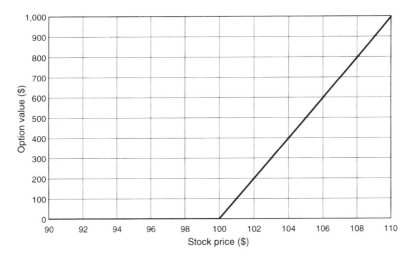

Figure 3.1 Value of option with exercise price = $100 on expiry

We see that the situation is very similar to that of a convertible bond. Above a certain price (the exercise price) the gradient of the straight line is a constant 100—the holder of the call option is exposed to 100 shares of IBM. Below the exercise price the gradient is zero—the holder is not exposed to the IBM share price at all. The only difference is that below the certain price, the convertible bond returns a lump sum, but a call option returns nothing.

In the above example we calculated the value of an option by assuming that the holder would exercise, take delivery of, and sell stock. In practice this is often not necessary. There is a well-established market in the options and in a real life situation the option could be sold for its intrinsic value. So if the stock price were $106 then the $100 strike call option could be readily sold for $600 or $6 per share. There is usually no need to go through the process of calling the stock.

3.2 OPTIONS TERMINOLOGY

Exchange traded stock options are usually listed with three, six and nine months of life and with various exercise prices. As time passes options expire (some worth something and some worthless) and so the exchanges usually list new ones.

A call option whose exercise price is below the current stock price is referred to as being **in-the-money**. A call option whose exercise price is above the current stock price is referred to as being **out-of-the-money**. A call option whose exercise price is equal to or nearly equal to the current stock price is referred to as being **at-the-money**. Most exchanges continually list options so there is at least one in-the-money and one out-of-the-money option for each **expiry cycle**.

In the definition of a call option above the expression "on or before a given date" means that the option is **American style**. This means that the holder can, if so wishing, exercise early and need not bother waiting until the final day. There are some options that can only be exercised on the expiry day. Such options are termed **European style**. In most instances the pricing difference between the two types is zero or small.

Call options can obviously be very profitable investments. As an example, in the situation above with IBM stock trading at $102 in the market, the in-the-money three-month call option with an exercise price of $100 may be priced at something like $3.50 per share. Option prices are always quoted on a per share basis. However, each IBM option is a contract for 100 shares and so one option would cost $100 \times 3.50 = \$350$. In this book we will always refer to the price of an option on a per share basis. For continuity we will always assume that option contracts are for 100 shares. Accordingly an option value or price will sometimes be referred to as $3.50 and sometimes $350. We say that this option is already $2 in-the-money, meaning that if it were immediately exercised one could recoup at least the difference between the market price and the exercise price. This in-the-money-ness is known as **intrinsic value** for obvious reasons. The difference between the intrinsic value and the option price, in this case $3.50 - \$2.00 = \$1.50$, is known as **time value**. Time value is what will be lost if the stock price remains completely unchanged between the purchase of the option and expiration. Time value is the money the speculator has at risk if the stock price stays constant. It is of course possible to lose more than the time value if the stock price falls.

This book is not intended as a detailed guide to option markets or option strategies and the interested reader is referred to the many excellent texts available.

3.3 PROBABILITY, AVERAGES, EXPECTED PAYOFFS AND FAIR VALUES

In order to understand the complexities of the pricing derivatives prior to expiry it is helpful to consider the concepts of calculating averages and following certain probabilistic arguments. All that follows can be done with simple arithmetic. No formal mathematics is required.

Consider entering a casino and playing the following simple game. You throw one six-sided dice. The payoff is equal to the number of spots on the uppermost face when the dice comes to rest. If you throw a one then you receive $1, if you throw a two you receive $2 and so on. The maximum you can win on any one go is obviously $6 and the minimum is $1. The question is what should the casino charge you to play such a game if it does not require to make a profit or loss? Most readers will intuitively guess the correct figure of **$3.50**, but it is instructive to go through the process of calculating this "fair value". We refer to it as the fair value because if you pay more, in the long run you will eventually lose and if you pay less you will eventually win. Consider playing the game 6,000 times. If the dice is an unbiased one, you would expect in the long run that one-sixth of the throws will result in a one, one-sixth will result in a two, one-sixth will result in a three and so on. So in 6,000 throws one would expect 1,000 ones to turn up giving us back $1,000 \times 1 = \$1,000$. Similarly one would expect 1,000 twos, paying back $1,000 \times 2 = \$2,000$ and so on. Table 3.2 lists the complete details. We see that after 6,000 games one would

Table 3.2 Calculating the fair value using frequency

Result of dice throw	Probability of this outcome	Likely frequency of outcome with 6,000 throws	Likely pay back
1	1/6	$6,000 \times 1/6 = 1,000$	$1 \times 1,000 = \$1,000$
2	1/6	$6,000 \times 1/6 = 1,000$	$2 \times 1,000 = \$2,000$
3	1/6	$6,000 \times 1/6 = 1,000$	$3 \times 1,000 = \$3,000$
4	1/6	$6,000 \times 1/6 = 1,000$	$4 \times 1,000 = \$4,000$
5	1/6	$6,000 \times 1/6 = 1,000$	$5 \times 1,000 = \$5,000$
6	1/6	$6,000 \times 1/6 = 1,000$	$6 \times 1,000 = \$6,000$
Total		$= 6,000$	$= \$21,000$
Average			$\$21,000/6,000 = \mathbf{\$3.50}$

"expect" a total pay back of $21,000. This represents an "average" pay back of 21,000/6,000 = $3.50 per game. So if we played this game 6,000 times and each time paid $3.50 to participate, then we (and the casino) would break even. If we paid $4 to play each time, then we would be losing on average $0.50 per game or a total of 6,000 × 0.50 = $3,000. If we paid $3.20 then we would be making on average $0.30 per game or a total of 6,000 × 0.30 = $1,800.

In this example we considered playing the game 6,000 times because 6,000 conveniently divides by 6. We could easily have used 60,000 or 6 million, the answer would be the same—the average payoff and hence the fair price is $3.50. Mathematicians refer to such "future averages" or "prospective averages" of, as yet, unrealised figures, as **expected values**. If you sit down to play this game a considerable number of times, you expect to get back an average of $3.50 per game. The interesting point about this and many other examples is that with any one throw you can never actually get the expected payoff—$3.50 is never paid out as the result of one throw; it is just the most likely long-run average that one will achieve.

In this case, since the dice is unbiased, all the possible outcomes are equally likely. Such a distribution of outcomes is termed **uniform**. When the distribution of outcomes is so simple, there is an easier method of calculating the expected or fair value. Rather than go through the complications of considering throwing the dice 6,000 times just assume that the dice is thrown 6 times. Since the individual outcomes are equally likely, assume that each one occurs once. Thus a one occurs once paying $1, a two occurs once paying $2 and so on.

Table 3.3 Calculating the fair value of a uniform distribution

Result of dice throw	Payoff
1	$1
2	$2
3	$3
4	$4
5	$5
6	$6
Total	$21
Expected value	21/6 = $3.50

This is outlined in Table 3.3. With the six throws, a total of $21 is paid out. $21 over 6 throws means 21/6 = $3.50 per game.

Now consider a slightly different game still using the same dice. This time, however, if a one or two is thrown, there is no pay back. What is the new fair price? Since the distribution is still uniform we can use the new simpler method outlined in Table 3.4.

So the new game has a lower expected long-run average of $3.00 per game. This is not surprising since two out of six throws (the one and the two) will result in no payoff. The type of payoff in Table 3.4 is somewhat like that of a call option on expiry. Some outcomes are zero and the rest increase linearly.

We now use this type of argument to see how it is possible to get an idea of how call options can be priced prior to expiry.

3.4   THE FAIR VALUE OF A CALL OPTION

We now consider a method by which we can calculate the price of a call option before expiry. We do this by making what initially looks like a very unrealistic assumption. The method follows on from the simple probabilistic ideas outlined above and although naïve, has the virtue of using no complex mathematics. The method also gives remarkably realistic option price profiles.

Table 3.4   Calculating the fair value of a truncated distribution

Result of dice throw	Payoff
1	0
2	0
3	$3
4	$4
5	$5
6	$6
Total	$18
Expected value	18/6 = $3.00

An at-the-money Option

Consider the purchase of a call option with an exercise price of $100
that expires in three months time. Today the stock price is $100 so the
option is at-the-money. What should one pay for the such an option?
We know that if the stock price rises significantly by expiry, we will
profit from the purchase. If the price rises to $105 then the option will
be worth $5. However, if the price falls to $95 then we will have lost
all the investment. For simplicity assume that on expiry the stock price
can only rise or fall by as much as $5. Furthermore assume that the
stock price can only be integral, i.e. it can only be at one of the following 11 values: $95, $96, $97, $98, $99, $100, $101, $102, $103, $104 or
$105. We also assume that each of these final 11 stock prices is equally
likely. If this were the case, the call option prices on expiry would be
$0, $0, $0, $0, $0, $0, $1, $2, $3, $4 and $5 respectively. Table 3.5 lists
all the possibilities.

  The situation is very much like the dice throwing example above
except that here there are eleven 11 likely outcomes. Consider playing
two "games". In one game, an investor repeatedly buys the stock at
$100, waits three months and then sells. Sometimes (one eleventh of
the time) the final stock price is at $105, sometimes it is at $104, etc. If

Table 3.5 Calculating the fair value of an at-the-money call
option.

Stock price today	Stock price on expiry ($)	Price of call option on expiry($)
	95	0
	96	0
	97	0
	98	0
	99	0
100	100	0
	101	1
	102	2
	103	3
	104	4
	105	5
Total	**1,100**	**15**
Average	**1,100/11 = 100**	**15/11 = 1.36**

the investor plays this game frequently enough, in the long run his average end price will be $100. The stock player will in the long run break even. The uniform distribution of stock prices ensures that the long run average will be $100. This example was deliberately constructed so as to introduce no bias in the option price.

In another game, an investor repeatedly buys the option (at a price yet unknown) and waits three months for expiry. Sometimes (one-eleventh of the time) the final pay back is $5, sometimes it is $4, etc. but often (6 times out of 11) the option expires worthless. Since each of the outcomes is equally likely, it is easy to calculate what the average option pay back is. Table 3.5 shows that the average option pay back is $1.36. In order for the option investor, like the stock investor, to break even he must pay $1.36 to play. If he pays more than $1.36 he will lose in the long run and if he plays less he will win. The fair value of the option under these simple assumptions is $1.36.

Before we continue it is worth looking at Table 3.5 again. In calculating the average stock price on expiry one did not need to go to the bother of adding up all the values of: $95 + $96 + ... + $105 to get the total of $1,100 and then dividing by 11 to get $100. A far simpler method would have been to note that the distribution of prices is perfectly symmetric around $100 and that this is the obvious middle or average price. With symmetric distributions, the middle (known as the median) is always equal to the average. This is not the case with the expiring option price distribution. The option prices on expiry are asymmetric. There are six values of zero and the rest increase linearly. The middle of this distribution is zero but the average is $1.36. The asymmetry is caused by the crucial element in an option contract. The fact that the holder has the right but not the obligation to get exposure to stock means that it is possible to opt out of a losing situation if stock prices fall.

In-the-money Options

Let us assume now that the stock price in question suddenly rises by $1 to $101. What will the price of the three-month $100 strike call option be? We now have a different situation. With the stock price at $101 it is now necessary to revise the future possibilities. For simplicity let us assume that the distribution stays symmetric about the new price and that again the prices on expiry will be integral up to a maximum

Table 3.6   Calculating the fair value of an in-the-money call option.

Stock price today	Stock price on expiry ($)	Price of call option on expiry ($)
	96	0
	97	0
	98	0
	99	0
	100	0
101	101	1
	102	2
	103	3
	104	4
	105	5
	106	6
Total	**1,111**	**21**
Average	**1,111/11 = 101**	**21/11 = 1.91**

of $5 up or down from $101. Accordingly the final possible stock-prices are set at: $96, $97, ..., $105, $106. Table 3.6 gives the new situation.

The fair value of the option is now $1.91. This is $0.55 more than the price of $1.36 when the stock price was at $100 and this seems reasonable. The price should be higher because there is more chance that the option will be worth something on expiry. There are now only five situations in which the option can expire worthless instead of the previous six. Also the maximum pay back is higher at $6 instead of $5.

Before we continue with the fair value calculations consider again the two situations above. When the share price was $100 the option price was $1.36. When the share price increased to $101 the option price increased to $1.91. It is easy to see the speculative attraction of options compared to stocks. Which would be more profitable, buying stock at $100 and selling at $101, or buying an option at $1.36 and selling at $1.91? The former investment returns a 1% profit whereas the latter returns a 40% profit. Note however, that although in percentage terms the option has increased more than the stock, in absolute terms the option has only increased by $0.55 compared to a $1.00 rise in the stock and this is a far more important observation.

Out-of-the-money Options

Let us assume now that the stock price in question instead of rising, falls by $1 to $99. The $100 strike call option is now out-of-the-money. Following the same logic as above, Table 3.7 gives the new fair value as $0.91 and this also seems reasonable since the possible outcomes for the option player are lower than when the stock was priced at $100.

We can repeat the above process for a number of various stock prices to get a complete picture of how the fair value of a call option price varies. The reader is invited to carry out the procedure for stock prices of $93, $94, ..., $106 and $107. The results appear in Table 3.8.

Figure 3.2 is a plot of the option price versus the stock price. Note the curved price profile. This is exactly how the prices of call options vary in reality. Even though we used a very unrealistic assumption about stock price distributions the resulting price curve is remarkably similar to certain call options.

1. **Far out-of-the-money call options are priced at zero**. With the stock price at or below $95 we know that the options can never be worth anything because of restricting the stock price rise to a maximum of $5. With very low stock prices, the call options will be worthless. At these very low prices the slope of the price curve will also be zero. In reality we find that

Table 3.7 Calculating the fair value of an out-of-the-money call option.

Stock price today	Stock price on expiry ($)	Price of call option on expiry ($)
	94	0
	95	0
	96	0
	97	0
	98	0
99	99	0
	100	0
	101	1
	102	2
	103	3
	104	4
Total	**1,089**	
Average	**1,089/11 = 99**	**10/11 = 0.91**

Table 3.8 Call option price before expiry versus stock price

Stock price today ($)	Call option price today ($)
93	0
94	0
95	0
96	0.09
97	0.27
98	0.55
99	0.91
100	1.36
101	1.91
102	2.55
103	3.27
104	4.09
105	5.00
106	6.00
107	7.00

this is also the case. Very far out-of-the-money options are priced at or near zero and are very insensitive to changes in the stock price.

2. **Far in-the-money call options are priced at intrinsic value**. With high stock prices, note that the option is priced with no time value. At say a stock price of $105, the option is priced at $5. Also, at these high prices, the sensitivity of the call option is very high. Above $105, the sensitivity is 100%.

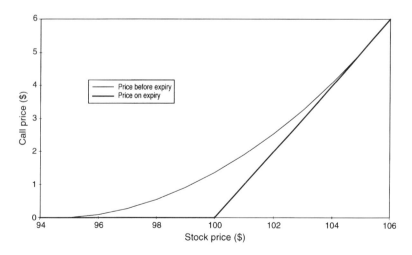

Figure 3.2 Call price before expiry

3. **The change from low price to high price is gradual and nonlinear**. The transition from a low value of $0 to a high value of $7 is smooth. Furthermore the slope of the curve gradually increases from 0 to 1. At $93 the slope is 0, at $100 the slope is 0.5 and at $107 the slope is 1.

All these characteristics are exhibited by call options in the real world.

3.5 THE NONLINEARITY OF CALL OPTION PRICES AND THE AVERAGING PROCESS

The numbers listed in Table 3.8 and displayed graphically in Figure 3.2 are the result of straightforward arithmetic. Each average or fair value is calculated by averaging 11 numbers. We consider the averaging process afresh. Beginning the discussion with the current stock price at $100, the average in Table 3.5 is calculated as follows:

$$\text{average with stock at \$100} = \frac{\overbrace{0 + 0 + 0 + 0 + 0 + 0}^{6 \text{ zeros}} + \overbrace{1 + 2 + 3 + 4 + 5}^{+\ 5 \text{ non-zeros}}}{11} = \frac{15}{11} = 1.36$$

When we move on to consider the situation with the stock price at $101 the new average is calculated as follows:

$$\text{average with stock at \$101} = \frac{\overbrace{0 + 0 + 0 + 0 + 0}^{5 \text{ zeros}} + \overbrace{1 + 2 + 3 + 4 + 5 + 6}^{+\ 6 \text{ non-zeros}}}{11} = \frac{21}{11} = 1.91$$

There are still 11 terms in the new total. The difference between the first and the second total is that a 6 has been added and a zero removed. This has meant that the total has increased by 6 or that the average has increased by 6/11 or 0.55 to 1.91.

Considering the next step up in stock price to $102, we calculate the average as follows:

$$\text{average with stock at \$102} = \frac{\overbrace{0 + 0 + 0 + 0}^{4 \text{ zeros}} + \overbrace{1 + 2 + 3 + 4 + 5 + 6 + 7}^{+\ 7 \text{ non-zeros}}}{11} = \frac{28}{11} = 2.55$$

The difference between the second and the third total is that a 7 has been added and a zero removed. This has meant that the total has increased by a further 7 or that the average has increased by 7/11 or 0.64 to 2.55.

We could continue this argument considering successively higher stock prices. At each step the total will contain one less zero and one extra number. The additional number also steps up by one unit. The net effect of this is that the total increases, in a nonlinear way. At each step the total increases by one more unit than the previous step. Since the total increases in an ever-increasing way so does the resultant average. And this is why we have the curved profile. It is the zeros in the averaging process that do it. Table 3.9 shows the arithmetic process in complete detail.

Note that once the current stock price increases above the $105 level, the totals (and hence the average) behave differently. After a price of $105 is reached there are no longer any zeros. Above $105 each new total still involves the addition of a new higher number but the one being removed is now non-zero. The one being removed is always 11 units lower than the one being added. Accordingly the total increases by a constant value of 11 and so the average increases by a constant value of 1. Above the price of $105 the rate of increase of the average remains constant. In graphic terms the ever-increasing upward-sloping curve flattens out to become a constant straight line.

As one considers lower and lower current stock prices the situation is the reverse. The number of zeros involved in the total increases until eventually it comprises all zeros. Below a stock price of $96 the totals and hence averages are all constant at a value of zero.

The properties exhibited by the option fair values are a direct result of an averaging process. When the different possible outcomes have an asymmetric distribution, the averages have a curved profile. In all of the above we assumed that each of the different outcomes was equally likely so that the arithmetic would be easy. It is possible, however, to show that whatever type of distribution one assigns to the different outcomes, the asymmetry will always produce a curved price profile with very similar characteristics. This means that it is possible to overlay a much more realistic stock price distribution and get a more accurate description of the option price profile.

Table 3.9 Detailed averaging process

Current stock price	Different possible outcomes											Total	Increase in total	Average
93	0	0	0	0	0	0	0	0	0	0	0	0	0	0.00
94	0	0	0	0	0	0	0	0	0	0	0	0	0	0.00
95	0	0	0	0	0	0	0	0	0	0	0	0	0	0.00
96	1	0	0	0	0	0	0	0	0	0	0	1	1	0.09
97	2	1	0	0	0	0	0	0	0	0	0	3	2	0.27
98	3	2	1	0	0	0	0	0	0	0	0	6	3	0.55
99	4	3	2	1	0	0	0	0	0	0	0	10	4	0.91
100	5	4	3	2	1	0	0	0	0	0	0	15	5	1.36
101	6	5	4	3	2	1	0	0	0	0	0	21	6	1.91
102	7	6	5	4	3	2	1	0	0	0	0	28	7	2.55
103	8	7	6	5	4	3	2	1	0	0	0	36	8	3.27
104	9	8	7	6	5	4	3	2	1	0	0	45	9	4.09
105	10	9	8	7	6	5	4	3	2	1	0	55	10	5.00
106	11	10	9	8	7	6	5	4	3	2	1	66	11	6.00
107	12	11	10	9	8	7	6	5	4	3	2	77	11	7.00
108	13	12	11	10	9	8	7	6	5	4	3	88	11	8.00
109	14	13	12	11	10	9	8	7	6	5	4	99	11	9.00

3.6   THE FAIR VALUE OF A LONGER-DATED CALL OPTION

In the above example we assumed that the stock price on expiry could only have one of 11 different values around the current stock price and that the option had three months to expiry. We now address the question of pricing a six-month call option on the same stock. Obviously the six-month option should be worth more than the three-month option but how do we go about a valuation using the same naïve method? The answer is simple. We assume that there are more possibilities for the stock price at the end of a six-month period than there are at the end of a three-month period. For simplicity let us assume that instead of restricting the stock price to up or down $5 we allow the price to be up or down $8. So there will be 17 final possible stock prices of: $92, $93, . . . , $107, $108 with 17 corresponding option prices of : $0, $0, . . . , $7, $8. It is left as an exercise for the reader to follow the same procedure as above and prove that the fair value is now $2.12. Using the same procedure, the fair values of the six-month option, at different stock prices, are given in Table 3.10 and Figure 3.3.

For comparison the three-month option is also given in Figure 3.3. The six-month option has the same characteristics as the three-month option. At most stock price levels the six-month option has a higher price than the three-month option. This makes sense. The two options have identical prices at very low and very high stock prices. This is entirely consistent with what is observed in reality.

Table 3.10   Six-month call option prices

Stock price today ($)	Call option price today ($)
90	0
92	0
94	0.18
96	0.59
98	1.24
100	2.12
102	3.24
104	4.59
106	6.18
108	8.00
110	10.00

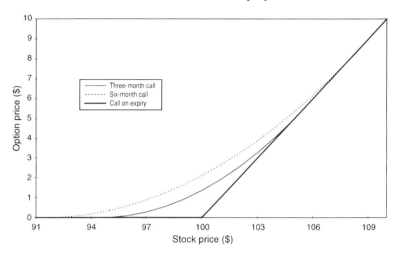

Figure 3.3   Call options with different expiry dates

3.7   INTRODUCING MORE REALISTIC DISTRIBUTIONAL ASSUMPTIONS

At the outset we stated that the assumption of a uniform stock distribution at some time in the future was unrealistic. If the stock is priced today at $100 we would not really assign equal probabilities to prices of $95, $96, ..., $105 in three months time. Most individuals would assign a higher probability to the current stock price and a lower probability to prices further away. Unless some extraordinary event occurs one would normally assume that the stock price in three months' time will be near the present price. Also it is not realistic to limit the stock price movement to a maximum of up or down $5.

There are many different mathematical models for stock price distributions and all assign higher probabilities to the current price and all allow for the possibility of very extreme moves. The most commonly used model assumes a **lognormal distribution** for the percentage changes. There is no need here to go into the mathematical complexities of this distribution but we note that the results of many empirical studies of financial price series support the lognormal distribution argument. Two individuals, **Myron Scholes** and **Fisher Black**, in 1973 solved the problem of calculating the expected value of a call option price based on the lognormal distribution. The popularity of the Black and Scholes technique has meant that it has almost become the generally accepted "correct" pricing model. Readers interested in a detailed description and derivation of the Black and Scholes model are referred to the many excellent mathematical texts. The model has such widespread use that most financial information services such as Bloomberg and Reuters freely provide option valuations using their techniques. The technique is so common in the currency markets that practitioners actually quote model parameters rather than prices. A copy of the model in its basic form is given on the disc supplied with this book.

So what is the effect of using a distribution different from our naïve uniform one? The lognormal distribution assigns more weight to the current stock price and lower weight to prices far away. Assigning lower probabilities to the extremes of a distribution essentially reduces the chance of realising a large option value on expiry and will have the effect of lowering the expected value. This is offset, however, by the fact that the lognormal distribution does allow for the possibility of very extreme moves. Figure 3.4 gives the price of a three-month call option using the "correct" lognormal distribution, i.e. the Black and Scholes model, and the one using our naïve uniform distribution.

Note the remarkable similarity of the two price curves. Both approach the horizontal (zero price) line and both approach the intrinsic value line. The curves differ somewhat between the extremes. The Black and Scholes (i.e. lognormal) curve is derived from a complex set of equations, whereas the naïve curve is the result of some

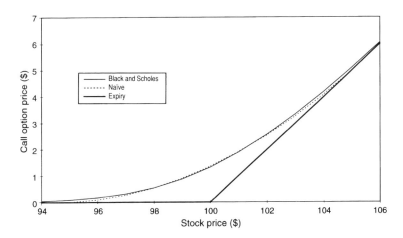

Figure 3.4 Black and Scholes versus naïve

very straightforward arithmetic. Both curves simply arise out of the asymmetric price profile on expiry, and the differences are due to associating different probabilities to different outcomes. The object of this chapter was to demonstrate, using a very simple argument, the reason behind the observed nonlinearity of option prices. It is not really necessary to understand the exact details of the price curve but just to understand why the curve exists at all.

3.8   INTRODUCING INTEREST RATE AND DIVIDEND CONSIDERATIONS

Throughout this chapter we have ignored the effect of interest rates and dividends on stock call options. In reality, stock options (particularly deep in-the-money options) are affected by interest rates. Other things being equal, if interest rates rise, stock call options increase in price. Also, other things being equal, if the underlying stock pays dividends, call options are cheaper. We do not intend to go into the complexities but give a number of examples in chart form. In Figure 3.5 we present the price curves for three three-month stock options assuming different interest rates and using the more appropriate Black and Scholes model. Note that in-the-money options are more sensitive to interest rate effects than out-of-the-money options. Interest rates have the effect of lifting the linear part of the price profile above the intrinsic value line. For the purposes of this book it is not

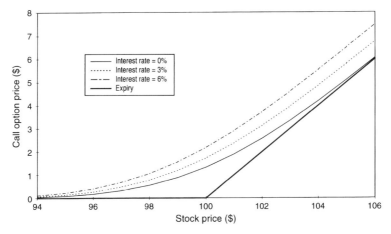

Figure 3.5   Interest rate effects on call option prices

necessary to expand on the interest rate effects but just to note that the curvature is still present, but shifted somewhat.

3.9 STOCK EXPOSURE OF CALL OPTIONS AND THE DELTA

We now need to look in detail at how the stock exposure of a call option varies. It is convenient for this and many other expositions to consider a longer dated option and so Figure 3.6 gives the price of a one-year call option with an exercise price of $100. For simplicity we have assumed that we are working in a zero-interest rate environment and that the option behaves perfectly according to the Black and Scholes model. This option will be used as the standard example throughout Chapter 4 and a detailed listing of the prices is given later. However, here special attention will be paid to three points of the curve A, B and C. The option prices, option contract values and stock exposures around these three points are given in Table 3.11.

Point A: With the Option Out-of-the-money

At point, A, with the stock price at $91.00, the option is priced at $2.30 so one option contract would be worth 100 × 2.30 = $230. If the stock

Table 3.11 Stock exposure of one-year call option

Point	Stock price	Change in stock price around point	Option price	Change in price around point	Option value	Change in value around point	Stock exposure (shares)	Delta
A	90.9 **91.0** 91.1	**+/−0.1**	2.27 **2.30** 2.33	**+/−0.03**	227 **230** 233	**+/−3**	**30**	**0.30**
B	98.9 **99.0** 99.1	**+/−0.1**	5.41 **5.46** 5.51	**+/−0.05**	541 **546** 551	**+/−5**	**50**	**0.50**
C	111.9 **112.0** 112.1	**+/−0.1**	13.98 **14.06** 14.14	**+/−0.08**	1,398 **1,406** 1,414	**+/−8**	**80**	**0.80**

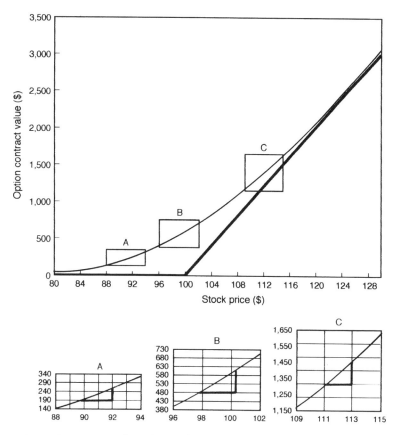

Figure 3.6 One-year call option value

price increases or decreases by a very small amount, say 10 cents or $0.10, we see that the price of the option increases or decreases by 3 cents ($0.03) and that the contract value will increase or decrease by $3. How many shares of the underlying stock would we need to replicate this change in value? The answer is 30 shares—30 shares times 10 cents equals 300 cents or $3. In Chapter 2 we showed that the stock exposure of an investment was equivalent to the slope of the value or profit and loss line. The value line here is not straight but curved. The slope and hence stock exposure are therefore constantly changing. For very small changes in the stock price, however, we can approximate the slope of the curve by drawing a tangent and estimating its slope. The insert in Figure 3.6 shows that the slope of the curve at point A is obtained from the small triangle drawn under the tangent. At point A,

not surprisingly, the slope is 30. Although the option under consideration is exercisable into 100 shares (on expiry), at the point A it is
behaving as if it were exercisable into 30 shares. The option value is
changing as if it were a portfolio of only a fraction of the true underlying share cover. This fraction is 30/100 = 0.30. This fraction is known
as the **delta** of the option and is one of the most important sensitivity
measures of an option.

Recall the imaginary black box portfolio in Chapter 2. Remember
that the contents of the portfolio were not disclosed but the price profile was given. At various points the portfolio had various exposures to
a certain stock. Also the stock exposure bore no relation whatsoever
to the price of the portfolio. We have a similar situation at point A. If
an investor buys one call option contract at A when the stock price is
$91 he will pay a total of $230. Once the stock price begins to move he
will discover that he is invested in something that behaves as if it contains 30 shares. An ordinary stock investor would have had to pay 30
× 91 = $2,730 to get the same exposure whereas the option investor
only has to pay $230. We say that the gearing or leverage is 2,730/230
= 12 (approximately). Also, like the black box portfolio, once the
stock price moves the exposure will also move.

Point B: With the Option Nearly At-the-money

At B the stock price is $99.00 and the option is almost at-the-money.
The price of the option has increased to $5.46 and so one contract
would be valued at $546. Also, we see that the slope of the curve and
stock exposure has increased to 50 shares. At point B the option is
behaving as if the holder is long of 50 shares. The delta here is 50/100
= 0.50. At point A the option had exposure to 30 shares and at B this
has increased to 50 without the option holder doing anything. This is
the fascinating aspect of call options. The actual exposure to the
underlying stock is increasing with the stock price increasing. It is as if
the holder is buying more shares as the price rises.

Point C: With the Option In-the-money

At, C, the curve is even steeper. The option is behaving as if it con-
tained 80 shares and so the delta is now 0.8. With the stock price this

high, the option price is beginning to respond much more to changes. At C the option catches 80% of the stock price movements.

Above Point C

It is easy to see that if the stock price were to continue to rise, the option price also continues to rise. As the stock price rises above C, the exposure or slope also rises but eventually tapers off to a constant maximum value of 100. At very high stock prices the delta approaches a constant 1.0. After a certain point (above $140 in this case) the change in value of the option exactly mimics the change in value of 100 shares.

Below Point A

If the reverse were to occur and the stock price fell, the option price and stock exposure would also fall. With falling prices the option delta also falls. If the price falls far enough the delta eventually drops to zero.

3.10   THE DELTA AS A SLOPE

In the above discussion the delta was defined as the ratio of the share exposure of the option to the number of shares the option could be exercised into. At point A, the delta was 0.30, at B the delta was 0.50 and so on. It is, however, possible to think of the delta of an option itself as being a slope. Consider Table 3.11 again and instead of concentrating on the changes in contract values look at the changes in prices on a per share basis. Around point A, if the share price moves 10 cents, the option price moves 3 cents. The ratio of these price movements is $3/10 = 0.30$, i.e. the delta. At point B, the ratio of the price movements is $5/10 = 0.50$, i.e. the delta. So we can directly deduce that the delta of an option is also the price sensitivity measurement. The delta is the rate of change of the price of the option with respect to the change of the stock price and as such must be the slope of the option price vs stock price curve given in Figure 3.7. It is easy to see that the slope of the price curve is near zero at low stock prices and is near one at high stock prices.

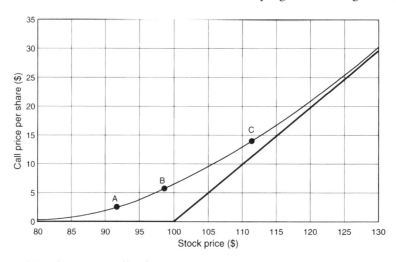

Figure 3.7   One-year call price

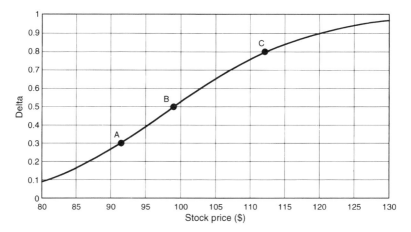

Figure 3.8   Delta of one-year call option

3.11   THE DELTA PROFILE

To the human eye, the price profile in Figure 3.7 is very smooth. The transition from low to high priced options is gradual. We know why the profile is curved—it is to do with the kink or asymmetry on expiry. But what about the slope (i.e. the delta) of the curve? Is the transition from zero to one equally smooth? It is possible to estimate the delta of the option at every value of the stock price. The delta of an option is also a product of the Black and Scholes model and details are given on the disc supplied with this book. As with the option prices, most information services freely provide estimates of deltas. Figure 3.8 is a plot of the delta of the option under consideration at various stock prices.

Points A, B and C are also highlighted in Figure 3.8. Note that the transition from a delta of near zero to near one is not uniform. The rate of change of the delta (the slope of a slope) is not constant. At low and high prices, the delta increases at a lower rate than at prices near the exercise price ($100). This is not immediately obvious from an examination of the original price curve in Figure 3.7. This characteristic of a non-uniform delta change is typical of all options and will be dealt with in more detail in the next chapter.

3.12 SUMMARY

In this chapter we demonstrated that the price of a call option before expiry is curved. This curvature is simply due to the uncertainty about the stock price on expiry. We know for certain what the option will be worth on expiry at all stock prices but we do not know what the stock price will be. By following a very naïve probabilistic argument and simple arithmetic it was possible to arrive at some sort of a curve. The very fact that the price is curved implies that the stock exposure changes with the stock price. Buying and holding a call option is like buying an investment involving a certain fraction of shares. The fraction is referred to as the delta and is also the slope of the price curve. Out-of-the-money calls have low deltas and are correspondingly not very responsive to the underlying share price. In-the-money calls have higher deltas and are much more responsive to stock price changes.

The delta and hence the stock exposure vary with the stock price. A fund manager holding call options whose underlying shares are increasing in value is essentially buying more shares on the way up. A fund manager holding call options whose underlying shares are decreasing in value is essentially selling shares on the way down. We finally stress again the importance of noting that the price paid for a call option is not the stock exposure. It is possible to have two options, one priced at 5 (with 3 days to expiry) and one priced at 20 (with 6 months to expiry), and the lower priced will have a considerably higher stock exposure.

4
The Simple
Long Volatility Trade

There are many different types of portfolios that will profit from volatility in a given stock price but by the far the most straightforward is that of being long a call option and short shares. As a lead into this discussion we consider a related but simpler strategy of stock outperformance.

4.1 OUTPERFORMING STOCK PORTFOLIOS WITH CALL OPTIONS

Here we show how an option investment can outperform a stock investment both in rising and falling markets. We show that this is possible by using the special curved call option profile. To do this we consider again the one-year call option illustrated in Figure 3.7. Recall that one option contract is exercisable into 100 shares but that the stock exposure is variable and depends on the underlying stock price.

We are going to compare the performances of two fund managers exposed to 50 shares of a certain stock. The stock in question is at a price of $99.00 and the one-year call option is priced at $5.46. One fund manager is long of 50 units of stock and the other is long of the one-year call option. From the discussion in Chapter 3 we note that the option fund manager is at point B in Figure 3.7 where the delta is 0.50 and the stock exposure is 50 shares. In the jargon of the options market we say that the two portfolios are **delta equivalent**.

Although the stock exposure of both managers is identical, the actual portfolio values are different. The stock manager has $50 \times 99 = \$4,550$ invested whereas the option manager has $100 \times 5.46 = \$546$

Table 4.1 Performance of option versus stock

Stock price	Stock portfolio (Long 50 shares)		Option price	Option portfolio (long one contract)		Difference
	Value Of shares = 50 × price	Change In value of shares from start point		Value of option contract = 100 × price	Change in value of option contract from start point	Outperformance of option over stock
93.0	4,650	−300	2.93	293	−253	+47
94.0	4,700	−250	3.28	328	−218	+32
95.0	4,750	−200	3.67	367	−179	+21
96.0	4,800	−150	4.07	407	−139	+11
97.0	4,850	−100	4.51	451	−95	+5
98.0	4,900	−50	4.97	497	−49	+1
98.9	4,945	−5	5.41	541	−5	0
99.0	**4,950**	**0**	**5.46**	**546**	**0**	**0**
99.1	4,955	+5	5.51	551	+5	0
100.0	5,000	+50	5.98	598	+52	+2
101.0	5,050	+100	6.52	652	+106	+6
102.0	5,100	+150	7.09	709	+163	+13
103.0	5,150	+200	7.69	769	+223	+23
104.0	5,200	+250	8.30	830	+284	+34
105.0	5,250	+300	8.95	895	+349	+49

invested. In this discussion we are only interested in what happens to both managers relative to their respective starting points and so we "zero out" the portfolios by removing these original investment values. Accordingly we subtract $4,550 and $546 from the respective portfolio valuations at subsequent stock prices. Table 4.1 and Figure 4.1 give the relative performance of the two fund managers if the underlying stock price rises or falls away from the value of $99.

We see that for very small changes in the stock price, the two portfolios perform almost identically. And this is what we would expect. We deliberately choose the number of shares in the stock portfolio so that the exposure would be identical to the option portfolio. We deliberately chose the slope of the stock portfolio profit and loss line to exactly match that of the option portfolio at point B. However, once we begin considering stock price moves of a larger magnitude, the situation is different.

Rising Stock Price

If the stock price rises from $99 to $101 the stock portfolio increases in value by $100. The corresponding option price rises from $5.46 to $6.52 resulting in an increase in contract value of $106. This represents an outperformance of $6 of the option portfolio over the stock portfolio. If the stock price rises even higher, the relative outperformance

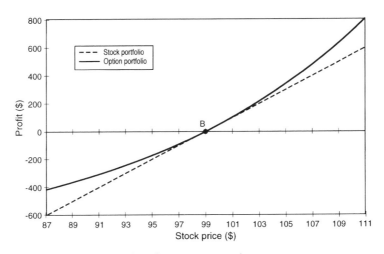

Figure 4.1 Performance of option versus stock

becomes even more marked. At a price of $105 the outperformance has increased to $49.

Falling Stock Price

If the stock price falls from $99 to $97 the stock portfolio decreases in value by $100. The corresponding option price falls from $5.46 to $4.51 resulting in a decrease in contract value of $95. In falling markets the option portfolio has lost value but less than the stock portfolio and so this still represents an outperformance of $5. If the stock price falls even lower the relative outperformance becomes even more marked. At a price of $93 the outperformance has increased to $47.

So it appears that the option fund manager outperforms the stock fund manager if the underlying price **rises or falls** and the reason is obvious from Figure 4.1. The option value curves above the straight stock value both sides of point B and it does this for the reasons explained in Chapter 3. This example may seem contrived in that the numbers were chosen so that the original stock exposures were identical, but it will always be possible to find an option portfolio to match initial exposures. And because option prices are curved, the above outperformance will always be achievable. So why does anyone ever get involved in real stock? Why not always use options? Using options does not of course guarantee a profit, but at least it appears always to do better than stock. The answer is that we are not telling the complete story. There is a **catch**. There is another aspect (that we have not mentioned yet) to consider and we will return to this later on.

It is correct to say, however, that a call option portfolio will definitely outperform a delta equivalent stock portfolio in the above manner if a significant price change is experienced.

4.2   THE LONG VOLATILITY DELTA NEUTRAL TRADE

We are now in a position to discuss in detail the mechanics of buying volatility. Say we believe that for the foreseeable future, the price of the stock in question will fluctuate excessively. Let us say that we know for sure that whichever way the price moves, it will be large and that there will be many swings in price. Unfortunately we have no idea which direction the price will move and when the direction will change. Of course not knowing which way the price is going to move is a serious disadvantage. We have to get into a position that will profit whichever way the market moves, up or down. This may seem a tall order but it is possible to achieve. We have to start with a position that is initially market neutral but that gets long if the market rises and gets short is the market falls.

If we look back at Table 4.1 and Figure 4.1 in which we compared the relative performance of two fund managers we have the answer. Both fund managers had to be initially long of the same amount of stock or to be in a position that, for small changes, had identical profit and loss changes. Unfortunately in that example, both individuals were long and could only benefit from rising markets. We want, initially anyway, to be market neutral.

The answer is to have a portfolio long of one option contract and to be simultaneously short 50 shares, i.e. to be long of the option manager's position and short of the stock manager's position. In this way the stock exposures of both components are identical but opposite in sign and must cancel out. We will refer to this as the long volatility or hedged portfolio. Calculating the change in value of this portfolio is straightforward. We simply reverse the signs of the stock portfolio values in Table 4.1. The resultant performance of the long volatility portfolio is shown in Table 4.2 and Figure 4.2.

In rising markets what is a profit for the stock manager is, of course, now a loss and these losses have to be subtracted from the option profits. In falling markets what is a loss for the stock manager is now a profit and these profits must be added to the option losses. In Figure 4.2 we have kept the stock profit and loss line displayed as a positive sloping line but in reality it is negative. Illustrated this way, it is easy to see that the net profit to the hedged portfolio will be the difference between the two value profiles and this is given separately in the lower chart. The net profit is simply the outperformance measure in Table 4.1.

Small Stock Price Moves

If the stock price rise is small, the option profits are almost completely wiped out by the short stock losses. If the stock price fall is small, the stock profits are almost completely wiped out by the option losses. So for small price moves up or down no profit or loss results. The position is perfectly hedged. The holder of such a position is said to be market neutral or delta neutral. It is as if the holder is not involved in the market at all.

The key to this position is getting the right mix of stock and option. The ratio here is 0.5—the delta. Any other ratio of stock to option would not be market neutral. It is left as an exercise for the reader to try different ratios and prove that losses or profits occur for small

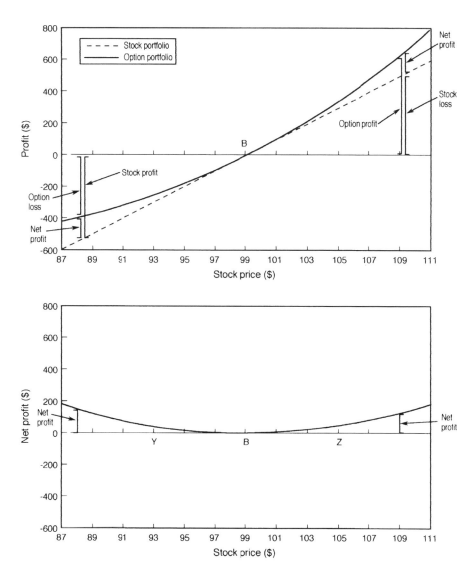

Figure 4.2   The long volatility trade

Table 4.2 The simple long volatility trade

Stock price	Stock component (short 50 shares)		+	Option component (long one contract)		=	Long volatility portfolio
	Value of shares = 50 × price	Change In value of position from start point		Option price	Value of option contract = 100 × price	Change in value of option contract from start point	Net profit of total portfolio
93.0	4,650	+300		2.93	293	−253	+47
94.0	4,700	+250		3.28	328	−218	+32
95.0	4,750	+200		3.67	367	−179	+21
96.0	4,800	+150		4.07	407	−139	+11
97.0	4,850	+100		4.51	451	−95	+5
98.0	4,900	+50		4.97	497	−49	+1
98.9	4,945	+5		5.41	541	−5	0
99.0	**4,950**	**0**		**5.46**	**546**	**0**	**0**
99.1	4,955	−5		5.51	551	+5	0
100.0	5,000	−50		5.98	598	+52	+2
101.0	5,050	−100		6.52	652	+106	+6
102.0	5,100	−150		7.09	709	+163	+13
103.0	5,150	−200		7.69	769	+223	+23
104.0	5,200	−250		8.30	830	+284	+34
105.0	5,250	−300		8.95	895	+349	+49

price moves. Because this ratio is so important in constructing hedged portfolios, the delta is also often referred to as the **hedge ratio**.

Large Stock Price Moves

If the stock price rises significantly, the option component always makes more than is lost by the stock component. If the stock price falls significantly, the profit on the short stock component always exceeds the loss on the option component. The bigger the move, up or down, the bigger the profit. After putting on this position we would hope for a very large market move and this is why the strategy is called the long volatility trade.

So whichever way the stock price moves, we always make a profit. That is the essence of the long volatility trade.

Figure 4.2 graphically demonstrates that the trade works simply because of price curvature. Note also that the resultant profit profile is also curved. It is, however, also useful to look at the strategy in stock exposure terms. We start off at B, with two positions with equal and opposite stock exposures, i.e. we start off market neutral. If the underlying stock price rises, the exposure of the option increases above the constant exposure of the short stock position and so the total portfolio automatically becomes long. The more significant the move the longer we get. If, however, the underlying stock price falls, the option exposure falls below the constant short stock exposure and so the total portfolio automatically gets short. The greater the fall the shorter we get. This is an ideal situation. We automatically become long in a rising market and short in a falling market.

Doing Nothing with the Long Volatility Trade

What happens if we instigate this trade at point B and we are fortunate to witness a large increase in the stock price to $105 or point Z? We will record a profit of $49 but for the moment the profit is only on paper and not realised. What happens if we get sucked into the belief that we might get lucky and that the stock price might continue to rise. If the price does continue to rise then we will certainly makc a larger profit, but what happens if the price falls all the way back to B? The profit vanishes. We could get lucky again and the price continue to fall to $93 or point Y at which point we would again record a profit, this time of $47. If this does happen and we still do nothing then the price could rise all the way back to point B resulting in no overall profit again. If we do not act, it is very likely that we will end up seeing a paper profit, then see it vanish, then see it return and so on. How do we lock in the volatility profits?

Rehedging the Long Volatility Position

Let us go back to the initial set up of the trade at B. If the first significant move is up $6 to $105 at Z we have our first mark to market paper profit of $49. The simplest and most straightforward way of locking this profit in is to **completely liquidate**. Sell the option at $8.95 and buy back the short stock at $105 and walk away from the trade keeping the (small) profit of $49.

This strategy of liquidation, however, may not make sense. There may be still more profit to be made out of the position. Consider another individual wishing to enter into the same strategy at Z. He believes that the market is going to continue to be volatile and wishes to capitalise on the option price curvature. The question is what ratio of stock to call option would be chosen at Z? At Z the delta is higher at 0.66. The new individual would buy one call option (exercisable into 100 shares) and sell short 66 shares. As with the first individual, if the market rises or falls significantly, a profit will result.

So why does our original investor not re-enter the market at Z with the new ratios? He could, but why bother ever to exit the trade at all? In a real market situation, each execution would cost money and so rather than liquidate and re-enter, why not just adjust the ratios of stock to option? At B the original individual was long one call option and short 50 shares. At Z, to be strictly market neutral, the mix should be long one call option and short 66 shares. The simplest action would be to sell a further 16 shares (at a price of $105) bringing the total up to 66. He now has the correct ratio of option to shares and is again delta neutral. The interesting point about this **rehedging** process is that the small profit of $49 is now locked in and the individual is back in business waiting for a significant move, up or down.

Where Does the Profit Come From in the Long Volatility Trade?

To demonstrate that the rehedging locks in the profit, consider the situation in which the stock price falls all the way down to $99 again, i.e.

back to point B. At B, the delta is again 0.50 and so the portfolio should only be short 50 shares. The portfolio is too short and accordingly to rehedge we simply buy back 16 shares at $99 and re-establish a new market neutral position. This new market neutral position of long one call option at $5.46 and short 50 shares at $99 is identical to the situation we started with. The only difference is that in going from B to Z and back to B all we really have done is sell 16 shares at $105 and buy them back at $99 giving a profit of $16 \times (105 - 99) = 96. This $96 profit is actually made up of the $49 made in going from B to Z and $47 in going from Z back to B. If we had not acted at Z and rehedged there would be no profit. The rehedging process locks in the original profit and sets up a situation in which further profits can be made.

Ideally we would like the stock price to oscillate between B and Z indefinitely. Each round trip would net us $96. But this is unlikely to happen. Let us consider the alternative scenario of the stock price falling from Z back to B but that this time the price continues to fall all the way down to point Y at $93. Remember that on the second pass through B we rehedged by buying 16 shares back, locking in a total profit of $96 and re-establishing a 50% hedge. With the stock price falling to Y, the option has the new lower delta of 0.34 and so the quantity of short stock should be only 34. Accordingly we rehedge by buying 16 of the 50 short shares back at $93. Finally, let us assume that the stock price moves all the way back to B. At B to get neutral again we must sell 16 shares (at $99) locking in a further profit of $16 \times (99 - 93) = 96 resulting in a total profit of $192. Figure 4.3 illustrates how, using this rehedging strategy, the profits gradually build up if the stock price continues to move from B to Z to B to Y to B, etc.

The upper chart in Figure 4.3 shows three different tangents to the curve at points Y, B and Z. The slopes of the three tangents represent the three different deltas and are 0.34, 0.50 and 0.66 respectively. As the stock price moves from one point to another the ratios of stock to option are adjusted according to these slopes. The lower chart shows the net profit to the trade. Beginning at B the profit is zero. As the stock price moves from B to Z a small profit of $49 accumulates in a curved fashion. At Z a rehedging transaction takes place re-establishing a delta neutral position. The price then moves back to B. The return journey produces a profit of $47 that builds on top of the original $49 making a total profit of $96. At B rehedging takes place again and the stock proceeds to Y adding further profits. As the stock price continues to move back and forth, we see that profits gradually build up. At each rehedging point the rate at which profits build up changes. This is because at each rehedging point a new neutral position is established. This process of continually rehedging to form new delta neutral positions is known as **dynamic hedging** for obvious reasons. Although this example is very contrived, it does illustrate clearly how the trade works.

It is easy to see why this is called the long volatility trade. The more the stock price moves and the more frequently the price reverses, the more scope for profits. A fascinating aspect of this trade is that by rehedging one is forced to sell in rising markets and buy in falling markets. One is always trading the opposite way to the general market trend. When the market is rising rapidly either due to some speculative story or due to some market participants being caught short, one is always selling. In a market crash situation when everyone is a panic seller, you are the buyer. Being the opposite way to the general market makes for easy executions.

So where do the profits come from in this trade? The answer is the

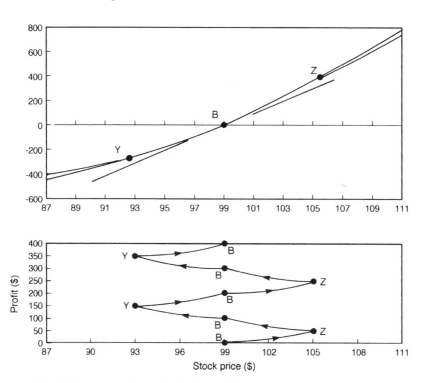

Figure 4.3   Rehedging at points Z, B and Y

rehedging. The rehedging process forces us always to be in the position of **buying low and selling high**.

What if the Stock Price just Continues to Rise?

Say the stock price instead of falling back from $105 continues to rise to $110 and then to $115 and so on. At $110 the delta is 0.76 and so further shares would be sold to bring the total short position of 76 units. As the price continues to rise, the delta also continues to rise and so more shares would be sold. There will come a point ($140 in this case) at which the delta reaches the maximum of 1.0. At this point the portfolio will consist of one option contract and short 100 shares. At this point the option value will be increasing exactly in line with the decreasing stock value and no further profits will be enjoyed. At this high stock price there is no more curvature left in the option price profile. It is important to note that one never gets into the situation of being net short. One never shorts more than 100 shares. The continual rehedging will have locked profits in on the way up but the overall profit to the trade, although positive, will be small.

What if the Stock Price Continues to Fall?

In a continually falling market, we would be constantly rehedging by buying stock and thus reducing the overall short, all the way down. If the stock falls to a sufficiently low price ($70 in this case) the delta will be zero by which point we would have bought back all the short stock. In this case, the final portfolio would consist of a worthless option and no stock. At very low prices the option has no more curvature and so provides no scope for further profit. The continual rehedging will of course have locked in profits on the way down but as with a continually rising market the overall profit to the trade, although positive, will be small.

What Type of Stock Price Movement is Best?

It is obvious from the above discussion that the type of stock price behaviour that would produce the most profit from this strategy is that of a continually oscillating one. Although the trade will still produce positive results in continually rising or falling market, far more profit will result with large gyrations.

Where is the Catch?

The reader has probably guessed already that there must be something wrong here. There must be a catch in the long volatility trade. It cannot be possible to end up with a situation that will always yield a profit. In the above examples with the stock price moving from B to Z to B to Y, etc., we have made one assumption that was convenient in order to explain the idea behind the trade. The assumption was that as the stock price moved backwards and forwards, **time stood still**. We assumed that the option was not getting any older. We assumed that the option price profile remained fixed for ever. In this way, every time the stock price passed through a given point, we could assume that the option price was always the same. This is, of course, not usually the case.

Unless the stock price moves from B to Z to B to Y, etc., 500 times a day we cannot assume that the option price profile remains the same. In reality it would take time to get from one price to another. In the process, other things being equal, the option will have lost some time value. **And that is the catch**. Every day that passes will cause the entire option price profile to decay slightly towards the kinked expiry price profile. We should really go back through the above examples and put the proper option price in each time we rehedge. Time decay will reduce the profits to the trade and in some cases cause a net loss. The strategy is still valid but only in the right circumstances. The trick is being able to identify the right circumstances. We return to this question later.

4.3   THE EFFECTS OF TIME DECAY—THETA

The loss of value of an option due to time passing is so important to market participants that it has been given a special name—**theta**. As time passes we say that an option suffers time decay or theta decay. Theta, like delta, is another sensitivity measure. Delta measures the sensitivity of an option with respect to the underlying share price and theta measures the sensitivity with respect to time. The one-year call option in question will, with the passage of time, become a nine-month option, then a six-month option and so on. Figure 4.4 shows how the value of the option varies with respect to the stock price at various times to expiry. A specific subset of points for later reference is also shown in Table 4.3.

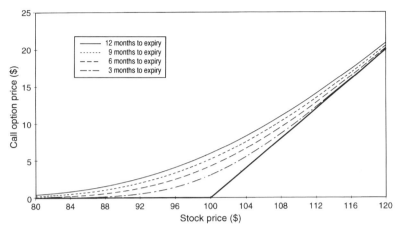

Figure 4.4 The effect of time decay on call options

Note that all option price profiles are curved and that the curves gradually collapse towards the expiry boundary. By considering various fixed stock prices it is possible to observe which options suffer the most time decay. The distance between the curves represents the extent of the time decay at each stock price. The curves are furthest apart with the stock price near the exercise price and most bunched together at the extremes. It is clear that the near-the-money options suffer the most time decay. As one moves further away from the exercise price, the effects of time decay get smaller and smaller. Deep out-of-the-money or deep in-the-money options have virtually no

Table 4.3 The effect of time decay on call options

Point	Stock price	12 months to expiry	9 months to expiry	6 months to expiry	3 months to expiry
	91	2.23	1.70	1.05	0.38
Y	93	2.93	2.27	1.52	0.67
	95	3.67	2.95	2.12	1.12
	97	4.51	3.75	2.86	1.74
B	99	5.46	4.68	3.76	2.56
	101	6.52	5.73	4.80	3.60
	103	7.69	6.90	5.99	4.83
Z	105	8.95	8.19	7.31	6.24
	107	10.31	9.58	8.76	7.82
	109	11.75	11.07	10.32	9.52
	111	13.27	12.64	11.98	11.32

time decay at all. This observation might tempt one to think that the solution for the long volatility player is to get involved only in those options with little or no time decay. However it is not that simple. The very options that have no time decay also have very little price curvature. And we need price curvature for the volatility trade. Options with the most curvature unfortunately suffer the most time decay. Again we return to this subject later.

Time decay can, and often does, ruin the long volatility trade. When we put this trade on we hope to experience price movements. Every day that the underlying price stays still is a day of time value lost. If the market one is involved in becomes completely stagnant then the losses due to time erosion can build up. Long volatility traders in such situations talk of "bleeding to death" through theta. It is instructive to see what degree of volatility or price movement is necessary to cover the cost of time decay. There are a number of ways of looking at this issue and, to illustrate just two, we return again to the initial situation outlined above. At the start, the portfolio contains one one-year call option priced at $5.46 and short 50 units of shares at $99. We are at point B.

Movement in One Direction

Consider the price moving from B to Z, a change of $6. If this happens instantaneously we know we will make money. But what if the move takes two weeks or two months? As an extreme example Figure 4.5 and Table 4.3 show the situation if the move takes three months. We see that with the stock price at $105 the option, which now only has nine months of life left, will be priced at $8.19 (not $8.95). The option value curve has slipped down so much that the profits are not enough to cover the stock losses. The straight stock line value now sits above the option value and this means that there is an overall loss. The new option contract value is $100 \times (8.95 - 8.19) = \$76$ lower than the one used in the naïve description of the trade without time value considerations. So what was a profit of $49 turns out to be a profit of $49 - \$76 = -\$27$, i.e. a loss. So what sort of price move in one direction do we need to make a profit? It is clear from Figure 4.5 that if the price had moved as far $106 in the three months then the trade would break even. If the price had moved higher then a profit would result. One can follow a similar argument with a down move. By plotting the option value curves for various time horizons it is possible to

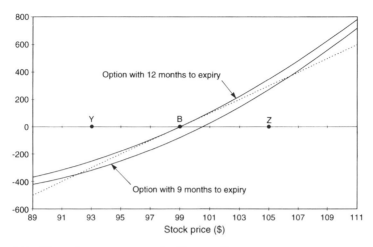

Figure 4.5   Time decay versus volatility profits

get an idea of how much the underlying has got to move to make a profit.

Price Swings

Another exercise can give one an idea as to how many price swings (with rehedging) are necessary to cover future time decay. Consider Table 4.3 again. Say the price of the underlying moves in the original contrived fashion of B to Z to B to Y, etc. Above we calculated that each trip from B to Z to B generated a profit of $96. If this trip took three months we see that the option at B would now be priced at $4.68, a drop of $5.46 − $4.68 = $0.78 or $78 for one contract. The volatility and rehedging made $96 but time value cost $78, so the net profit would be $96 − $78 = $18. One can repeat this exercise for various different scenarios to get an idea of what type of price swings one would need to make a profit.

The Frequency of Rehedging

In the example under consideration we rehedge every time the stock price moves $6. What if however, starting at B, the stock price never quite makes it to Z or Y but always just falls short of the rehedging point? No rehedging will mean no rehedging profits and since we are now considering a more realistic situation of option time decay, we will actually suffer losses. At the other extreme, consider the situation of the stock price swinging through point B much more violently each time. Say the stock price continues to move well past Z and Y before returning to B. Here we should obviously hold off rehedging until the stock price reaches the maximum and minimum of each swing. In this way each rehedging transaction will produce more profit. The problem is that we do not know how far the stock price is going to move. If we did we would not be bothering with this trade.

The problem reduces to one of judgement. Rehedging more frequently will certainly capture profits due to small price swings but has the disadvantage of missing out on the really large profits obtained with large price swings. Rehedging less frequently gives more scope for the large profits but will mean that the little profits associated with smaller price swings will be missed.

Two points to consider are the costs of rehedging and the likely time decay. In reality it is unlikely that one would bother with a portfolio containing only one option. A more realistic position would be, say, long 100 options and short 5,000 shares. With a bigger portfolio, rehedging can be done by adjusting the option or stock size, and costs such as the bid to offer spread, taxes and commissions will dictate which side to adjust. The chosen rehedging strategy will be a question of compromise. If the dealing costs are high (as with options on stocks) one has to wait for a significant price move to justify the transaction charges. If the dealing costs are low (as with options on futures) then rehedging can take place relatively frequently.

4.4   AN ALTERNATIVE VIEW ON OPTION FAIR VALUE

In Chapter 3 we talked of the fair value of an option and explained it in terms of a long run average. The analogy of playing a dice game was used to illustrate the concept of a probabilistic fair or expected value. In order to calculate the fair value one needed to have some idea of the different possible stock prices on the option expiry date. On expiry, it is a very easy matter to find the value of the option since, if it is in-the-money, it is worth the intrinsic value and, if it is out-of-the-money, then it is worth nothing. By "overlaying" these different expiring outcomes with a given stock price distribution it was a simple matter to come up with the expected value. We interpreted this expected value as being equal to the price one would pay for the option if, in the long run, we wanted to break even. The notion of long run here can be thought of in two ways:

1. In one, the option player repeatedly buys the option at the fair price and waits for expiry. Some of the time the option will end up being worth something and some of the time the option will end up worthless. If the player always pays the fair value his "winnings" will just cover his bets—he will break even.
2. In another interpretation one can think of the option player being offered a large number of different options all expiring on the same day in the future. If the player buys all of the options in one go and pays the correct fair value for each, then the net proceeds, when they all expire, will just match his total outlay—he will break even.

In both of these interpretations of the option fair value, we assume that the player buys and holds until expiry. Between the purchase date and the expiry date, the player simply looks on as the price of his position changes every day, but he never acts. In this interpretation of fair value the option participant plays a passive role. He either gets lucky with the stock price rising significantly or loses his stake.

The long volatility strategy now allows us to think of yet another concept of option fair value. Consider an individual setting up a delta neutral portfolio as outlined above and waiting for some volatility. Assume that the dealing costs are very small or zero. With no costs the long volatility player can afford to rehedge as frequently as he likes. Say he makes an arbitrary rule that he will rehedge each time the underlying price moves some small amount, say 10 cents. Will the player win or lose?

The answer depends on the price originally paid and the subsequent volatility experienced. If the price paid is low and the volatility is high, the player will win overall. If the price paid is high and the actual volatility is low then the player will lose. If the individual in question executes this trade on many occasions there will be a long-run average rehedging revenue. If this long-run revenue exactly matches the price paid, then we can say that the option price was fair in volatility terms. This, then, gives us another way to see if an option is expensive or not.

Which is the correct fair value to use? The two approaches to fair value are completely different. The former is passive—a simple buy and hold to expiry. The latter is active and involves continual dynamic rehedging. What is interesting is that it turns out that both approaches give the same answer. There is only one fair value but two different interpretations and the reason is not as complicated as it first seems. The key to understanding why these two different approaches give the same fair value lies in looking at the underlying stock price distribution in more detail. In Chapters 2 and 3 we used different models of stock price behaviour to explain different concepts.

In Chapter 2 we talked about measuring volatility. To illustrate how volatility was measured we considered how a certain stock price evolved from day to day. It was shown that volatility could be thought of as being a function of the sequence of daily price changes. We were not interested in where the stock price eventually went, just how it got there. In measuring volatility we were only interested in the magnitude of the positive and negative price changes.

In Chapter 3 we talked about the fair value of a call option and showed why the price profile should be curved. To do this we looked at a different aspect of the underlying stock price distribution. The fair value was shown to be a simple probabilistic average of the option prices on one day—the expiry day. The expiring option price is a direct function of the stock price on the expiry day and so we only required information about the stock price distribution on this one day. This approach completely ignores the path taken to expiry; it just uses the final expiry day price.

That is the difference in the two approaches. The static fair value model uses information about the stock price distribution on the one day in the future, whereas the long volatility fair value uses information about the day-to-day price fluctuations and completely ignores the future expiring price. Both approaches will give the same fair value if one assumes the same underlying stock price distribution. If we assume that the relevant distribution is lognormal and that the dispersion measure used is set equal to the expected volatility, then both fair value methods give identical results. If the volatility input into both models is high (low) then both fair values will be high (low). The volatility of the day-to-day price changes directly affects the distribution of prices on expiry. If the volatility is high then the distribution of stock prices on the one future expiry day will be very dispersed. If the volatility is high, then there will be a much higher chance of the expiring option ending up deep-in-the-money and being worth a considerable sum. So an option on a highly volatile stock should have a higher fair value even when one considers the static buy and hold strategy.

There is one final conceptual point to make on the two approaches to fair value. Say we know for sure that the stock in question will exhibit a volatility of 15% for the foreseeable future. We consider two individuals buying a one-year call option and paying the correct fair value that has been calculated using the Black and Scholes model with a volatility value of 15%. The first individual follows the buy and hold strategy and the second executes the delta neutral long volatility strategy. Say the stock price at the start is $99 and that the exercise price is also $100. The option in question happens to be the one used throughout this chapter so we know the price. It is $5.46 or $546 per contract. Both individuals should in the long run break even. Say the stock price on expiry is $90. The buy and hold player will have lost his entire stake of $546 but the volatility player will have recouped his $546 outlay through all the rehedging profits. The first individual will have lost 100% of his investment but the second will have broken even. And both paid the correct fair value. How can this be? Consider the individuals being given a second attempt at the same investment strategies. This time the stock price might end up at say, $114 in which case the option will end up being worth $14 or $1,400 per contract. The first individual will end up with $1,400 whereas the second will end up with $546. In this second attempt the buy and hold strategy makes 1,400 − 546 = $854 and the volatility strategy broke even. So that is the real difference in the two approaches to fair value. In the first approach, breaking even refers to a long run average and in the second breaking even means breaking even every time.

4.5   VOLATILITY AND VEGA

The Black and Scholes model is a complex equation that requires certain inputs. These inputs are usually referred to as parameters and for non-dividend paying stock options they are: (1) the stock price, (2) the exercise price, (3) the time to expiry, (4) the interest rate (if relevant) and (5) the volatility of the stock price. Like all mathematical models, the values of the output are only valid if the values of the inputs are correct. If there is any uncertainty or error associated with the input values then this will be reflected in the output. The first three variables are directly observable and the fourth, although not

Table 4.4 Vega—the effect of volatility on one-year call option

Stock price	Call option prices with volatility of				
	5%	10%	15%	20%	25%
91	0.06	0.88	2.30	3.93	5.66
93	0.16	1.32	2.93	4.69	6.50
95	0.39	1.89	3.67	5.52	7.40
97	0.82	2.61	4.51	6.44	8.37
99	1.52	3.49	5.46	7.44	9.41
101	2.54	4.53	6.52	8.52	10.51
103	3.87	5.72	7.69	9.67	11.67
105	5.45	7.06	8.95	10.91	12.89
107	7.21	8.54	10.31	12.21	14.17
109	9.09	10.12	11.75	13.58	15.50
111	11.04	11.81	13.27	15.02	16.89

fixed, is usually fairly stable over the life of an option. The volatility, however, is not directly observable and one has to use a historic estimate or use subjective judgement. If the volatility parameter used is too high (low) then the model will give a high (low) fair value. Table 4.4 and Figure 4.6 illustrate the effect of using various volatility inputs for the one year call option in question.

The sensitivity of option prices to changes in volatility is similar to the sensitivity to time. Near-the-money options are most sensitive and

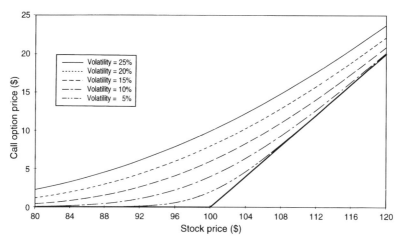

Figure 4.6 Vega—the effect of volatility on one-year call option

deep out-of-the money and deep in-the-money options are less sensitive. The figures illustrate the importance of getting the volatility right. The standard long volatility trade was explained using a fixed volatility of 15%. At the start with the stock price at $99 the option was priced at $5.46. If immediately after putting this trade on, the market priced all one-year options as if future volatility was only going to be 10% we see that the option price would immediately drop to $3.49 resulting in a loss without anything really happening. The sensitivity of option prices to changes in volatility is so important to market participants that it has been assigned a special symbol. The rate of change of an option price with respect to volatility is known as **vega**. Vega usually is defined as the change in option price caused by a change in volatility of 1%. At $99 the option in question has a vega of $0.40, at $120 a vega of $0.20 and at $80 a vega of $0.13. The vega of an option not only varies with the underlying stock price but also with time to maturity. Other things being equal, shorter dated options are less sensitive of volatility inputs—shorter-dated options have lower vegas. This is best illustrated by considering the variation in the option price over time at a fixed stock price but with different volatilities. Figure 4.7 shows the situation for at-the-money options. In graphical terms the vega of the option is equal to the distance between the 15% curve and either the 14% curve or the 16% curve. Note that as the time to maturity decreases, the curves converge. As time passes options become less sensitive to volatility changes or uncertainty in

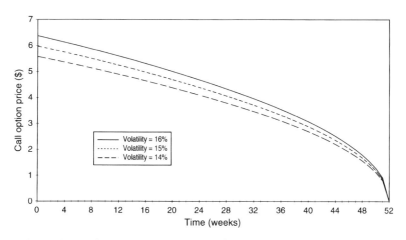

Figure 4.7 Vega of at-the-money call option

volatility estimation. Accurate volatility estimation is very important for very long-dated options and virtually irrelevant for very short-dated options.

4.6 IMPLIED VOLATILITY

It should be obvious by now that the value of the volatility parameter is crucial to the long volatility player. If one believes that future volatility is going to be 15% then with the stock price at $99, the break-even option price is $5.46. To make a profit one would really only get involved at a lower price or hope that future volatility will be higher than 15%. In the jargon of the market we say that the price of $5.46 is implying a future volatility of 15% or that 15% is the **implied volatility** of the option. By buying the option at $5.46 one is in essence paying up front for all the future rehedging profits associated with a stock price volatility of 15%. We say that we are **buying volatility at 15%**.

Consider now another situation. Another stock is priced at $109 that also has a one-year call option with an exercise price of $100. The option is offered at a price of $10.12. Examination of Table 4.4 shows that this price implies a volatility of only 10%. This option only requires a future stock price volatility of 10% to break even. If the two stocks in question are likely to exhibit similar volatility we can say that the option at $10.12 is cheaper than the one mentioned above priced at $5.46. The new option, although more expensive in dollar terms, is cheaper in volatility terms than the original one. So the implied volatility can be used as a measure of relative value. Options with different times to maturity, different stock prices and different exercise prices can be compared by simple reference to the implied volatility.

How does one calculate the implied volatility? The interested reader is referred to the relevant section on the disk supplied with this book. As with most calculations involving options no one ever really has to go to the bother of deriving implied volatilities since most information services provide on-line live values. However, the process is relatively straightforward. As mentioned above, the first four inputs into the model are known; the only unknown is the volatility. What is known, of course, is the market price of the option. In order to find the implied volatility one proceeds as follows. Substitute all the four known values into the model. Try substituting any volatility value, say

25%, and calculate the model price. Ask the question: is the model value the same as the market value? If the answer is yes then the implied volatility of the option is 25%. If the answer is no then try another value, say 24 or 26%, and repeat the procedure. Eventually one will arrive at a volatility that will give a model price that exactly matches the market price. As an example let this be 12%. This then is the implied volatility of the option. We say that the market price of the option is implying (if the model is valid) that the future volatility is going to be 12%. This procedure of trying various input values to match output prices may seem cumbersome and crude but in reality this is not so. There are well-known mathematical techniques that produce rapid and accurate results.

4.7 THE IMPORTANCE OF CURVATURE AND GAMMA

In the imaginary situation in section 4.2 in which the stock price conveniently oscillated back and forth, we deliberately chose the centre of oscillation as point B. The trade profits from volatility and only really works because of the option price curvature. And the price profile is only curved because of the kink on expiry. It should be obvious that for a given stock price move, say $x\%$, the more curved the profile, the more significant the rehedging profit. An alternative way of expressing the same idea is that one can achieve the same rehedging profit with a smaller stock price move using an option with a more marked degree of curvature. The long volatility player is always looking for low-priced curvature. Curvature is so important in the option market that it also has been assigned a Greek letter—**gamma**. This concept is best demonstrated by considering two imaginary option curves in Figure 4.8.

The two curves in Figure 4.8 have been specially chosen to have the same slope at point B just to illustrate the point. Curve (2) pulls away from the tangential straight line faster than curve (1) and would obviously produce higher rehedging profits. We can also use Figure 4.8 to loosely define curvature in terms of gradients. It is clear that at point B the gradients of both curves are identical but that at lower stock prices curve (2) has a smaller gradient than curve (1) and that at higher stock prices curve (2) has a higher gradient than curve (1). As the underlying stock price increases both curves have increasing slopes but curve (2) is increasing at a faster rate. And that is a defini-

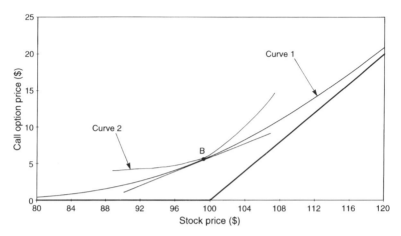

Figure 4.8 Option price curvature—gamma

tion of curvature—the rate of change of the slope. Since the slope of the curve is the delta we say that the curvature is the rate of change of the delta. **The gamma of an option is the rate of change of the delta**. This may at first seem complex since the delta itself is a rate of change. The delta is the rate of change of the option price with respect to the underlying stock price. So the gamma is the rate of change of the rate of change of the option price with respect to the stock price. Rather than try to think at various levels of rates of change it is easier just to think of the gamma in terms of curves and remember that high gamma options provide more rehedging profits.

A graphical representation of the gamma of a one-year call option is given in Figure 4.9. The first panel shows the option price. The second panel shows the delta or the slope of the first curve. The third panel shows the gamma or the slope of the second curve. One can think of gamma in terms of the original price curve or the delta curve. In terms of the original price curve we can see that deep in-the-money and deep out-of-the-money, the price profile is nearly linear or has very little curvature. The maximum curvature is near-the-money. In terms of the delta profile we can see that the maximum slope occurs near-the-money and that at very high and low stock prices, the slope of the delta curve is small. Note also that the gamma of a long call option is a **positive number** and this is because as the underlying stock price increases so does the slope of the price curve. Upward-sloping price curves always have positive gammas.

The strict mathematical definition of gamma is the instantaneous

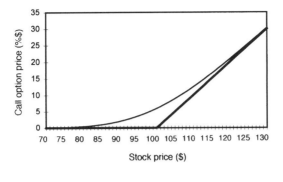

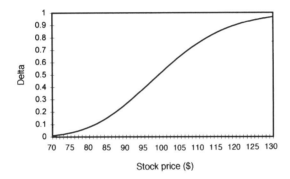

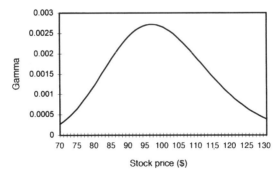

Figure 4.9   Option price—delta—gamma

rate of change of delta. In practice it is easier to consider the changes in delta caused by small stock price changes. The real use of gamma to the option trader and the volatility player is in the estimation of future rehedging activity. Gamma is the change in delta associated with a change in price of the underlying and so the gamma is also a measure of the rate at which we rehedge a delta neutral position. Table 4.5 illustrates the situation for a portfolio containing 100 options. Each option is exercisable into 100 shares and so for this portfolio all deltas and gammas are multiplied by $100 \times 100 = 10,000$. We arbitrarily define the gamma here as the change in delta due to a move of $0.10 in the underlying.

As an illustration of the meaning of gamma consider the $80 row. At this price the 100 options would require 789 short stock units to be completely delta neutral. At this price the gamma is 12.3 units and so small price changes of $0.10 would require rehedging by + or − 12 stock units. At a price of $95 the gamma is 27 units and so small price changes of $0.10 would require rehedging by + or − 27 stock units. The long volatility trade generates profits from the curvature and these profits are locked in by the rehedging process. So the gamma of the position is a direct measure of the potential profit due to volatility and often the term long gamma is used instead of long volatility. The term **long gamma** also refers to the fact that the gamma of the position is positive. We can see from Figure 4.9 and Table 4.5 that the most potential, the highest gamma, is near-the-money. Unfortunately these are the very options that suffer the most theta decay.

Table 4.5 Gamma of one-year call option

Stock price ($)	Option price ($)	Delta (a)	Gamma for $0.10 (b)	Stock exposure = 100 × 100 × (a)	Change in stock exposure due to $0.10 move = 100 × 100 × (b)
70	0.04	0.0106	0.00027	106	2.7
75	0.14	0.0327	0.00065	327	6.5
80	0.40	0.0789	0.00123	789	12.3
85	0.98	0.1566	0.00189	1,566	18.9
90	2.02	0.2652	0.00243	2,652	24.3
95	3.67	0.3948	0.00270	3,948	27.0
100	5.98	0.5299	0.00265	5,299	26.5
105	8.95	0.6555	0.00233	6,555	23.3
110	12.50	0.7613	0.00187	7,613	18.7
115	16.52	0.8430	0.00139	8,430	13.9
120	20.89	0.9016	0.00096	9,016	9.6
125	25.50	0.9409	0.00062	9,409	6.2
130	30.28	0.9659	0.00039	9,659	3.9

4.8 TIME DECAY EFFECTS ON DELTA AND GAMMA

All options before expiry have a curved price profile. At any point in time the slope of the curve, the delta, gives the equivalent stock exposure. At any point in time the curvature (the gamma) is the measure of how rapidly this stock exposure is changing. As time passes options decay in value and approach the expiring kinked price profile. It is instructive to consider in more detail how the delta and the gamma of various parts of the curve vary over time. One can do this without the traditional method of resorting to complex calculus but by simply looking at blow-ups of three parts of the option curves in Figure 4.10 and considering again the portfolio long of 100 options.

Out-of-the-money Options

For simplicity assume that as time passes the option stays out-of-the-money. We see that the slope of the curve and the degree of curvature gradually decrease to zero. Time passing causes the stock exposure (delta) and the rate of change of the stock exposure (gamma) to decrease. Running an out-of-the-money long volatility position to expiry would therefore involve gradually reducing the stock hedge. As expiry approaches, the scope for rehedging or delta readjusting would decrease.

In-the-money Options

The passage of time causes the slope of the curve to gradually increase. In the limit, the curve becomes coincident with the parity line. In the limit, the delta approaches 1.0 and the option becomes indistinguishable from stock. Also, the curvature gradually decreases. Running an in-the-money long volatility position to expiry would therefore involve gradually increasing the stock hedge until on expiry the longs and shorts would match one for one. As with out-of-the-money options, as expiry approaches, the gamma decreases and so the scope for rehedging would decrease.

Near-the-money Options

The most interesting aspect of near-the-money options approaching expiry is that the curvature increases as one gets nearer and nearer the

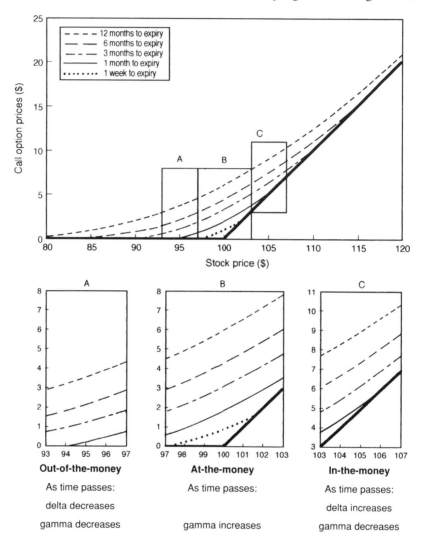

Figure 4.10 Time decay effects on delta and gamma

final kink and the scope for rehedging increases. Table 4.6 gives the maximum curvature points for the various options in Figure 4.10. With one year to expiry the maximum gamma is 27 and occurs at a price of $97. With one week to expiry this will have increased to 192 and occurs at a price of $99.8. With one year to expiry, a price change of $0.10 would require 27 stock units to rehedge but with one week to

Table 4.6 The maximum curvature points

Time to expiry	Stock price ($)	Gamma
12 months	97.0	27
6 months	98.5	38
3 months	99.0	54
1 month	99.5	93
1 week	99.8	192

expiry, the same stock price move would require 192 stock units. Expiring near-the-money options have large gammas and this is because the delta can swing from 0.0 when the option is slightly out-of-the-money to 1.0 when the option is slightly in-the-money. As an extreme example consider an option about to expire in one minute. At almost any price below $100, say $99.5, the option must be completely insensitive to changes in the stock price; the delta would be 0.0. At almost any price above $100, say $100.5, the option would behave completely like stock; the delta would be 1.0. If in the closing minutes of the expiry cycle the stock price moved up and down around the exercise price then the rehedging activity would be enormous. One second the hedge would be 10,000 short stock units and the next it would be zero. Every time the stock price increased slightly one would sell short 10,000 units of stock only to buy them back if the price fell slightly. This then would be the long volatility player's dream.

We summarise by noting that the simple picture given in Figure 4.10 illustrates, without the use of calculus, three aspects of call option price sensitivities:

1. The gradually collapsing price level shows the different degrees of time decay (theta).
2. The way the slope of the curve decreases (increases) for out-of-the-money (in-the-money) options illustrates the manner in which the sensitivity (delta) of the option price changes over time.
3. The curvature (gamma) or change in sensitivity is maximum near-the-money and increases as expiry approaches.

These effects are emphasised by illustrating the prices, deltas and gammas of the various options in the three panels of Figure 4.11.

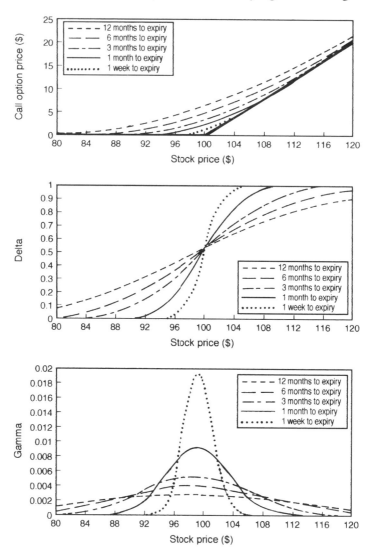

Figure 4.11 Time decay effects on delta and gamma

4.9 DELTA CONTOURS

Another way of representing the variation of deltas and gammas as time passes is a delta contour map. Figure 4.12 shows the points on a stock price versus time map where the option deltas are given fixed values. For clarity we show only 11 contours. Each contour maps out

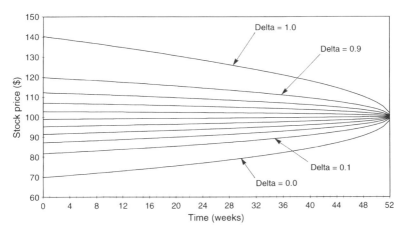

Figure 4.12   Fixed delta contours

all the points that have a given delta. The 11 contours correspond to deltas starting at 0.0 and increasing in equal units of 0.1 until 1.0. Along the lowest contour the delta is 0.0; along the second lowest contour the delta is 0.1 and so on. The highest contour corresponds to a delta of 1.0.

There are a number of ways of looking at this diagram. Consider a straight horizontal line drawn through the $90 price level. This represents the situation of the underlying stock price remaining constant at $90 until expiry. At the start (time = 0) with one year to go we can see that the option has a delta between 0.2 and 0.1. As time passes, if the stock price stays constant, the straight line enters lower and lower delta territory until after approximately 47 weeks (with 5 weeks to expiry) the line cuts into the 0.0 delta zone. As time passes the deltas of out-of-the-money options decrease. By considering a straight horizontal line drawn through the $110 price level one can see that exactly the opposite occurs. The line cuts through higher and higher delta contours eventually to enter the delta = 1.0 zone. As time passes the deltas of in-the-money options increase. This then reinforces the observations from the option price curves in Figure 4.10.

Plots such as Figure 4.12 can also demonstrate the way in which the rehedging activity alters as expiry approaches. If we plot the usual time series representation of the stock price on the same option contour map, we can see what is happening to the long volatility portfolio.

As the stock price moves over time the contours give a direct indication of the state of the portfolio. The portfolio is initially delta neutral but as the stock price rises or falls the contours can indicate the degree of non-neutrality. Say the initial delta is 0.5 and that subsequently the stock price begins to rise. As one crosses higher and higher delta contours the portfolio becomes increasingly unbalanced on the long side. There will be a point, depending on the rehedging strategy, at which rebalancing must take place. One can in fact use the contours to dictate when to rehedge. If we make an arbitrary rule that we only adjust the stock hedge each time the delta changes say by 0.10 then each time the stock price crosses one of the fixed contours we would rehedge. It is thus possible to see on a traditional stock price versus time chart when a rehedging trade occurs.

With one year to go the distance between the rehedging contours (in stock price terms) is large and there may be little activity. As time passes the contours converge and provided the stock price stays fairly near the exercise price of $100, the rehedging activity would increase. With one year to expiry a stock price move from $97 to $103 would cross one contour. The same move with only three weeks to expiry would cross seven contours. These plots also illustrate the importance of distance (in dollar terms) between the stock price and the exercise price at various times to expiry. With one year to expiry the stock price can be up to $40 from the exercise price and still the option has the possibility of providing useful rehedging profits. With only three weeks to expiry the useful range is reduced to $12.

4.10   THREE SIMULATIONS

We are now in a position to illustrate some simulations of the long volatility trade. Three different random price series were generated with varying underlying volatilities. It was assumed that the option in question is initially priced as if the future volatility is going to be 15%. Each series starts with the stock price set to $100 and the option is priced at $5.98. For simplicity we use the above trading rule and readjust only when the delta of the option changes by 0.10.

Figure 4.13 shows the situation when the underlying volatility experienced is high at 30%. The stock price crosses the contour lines many

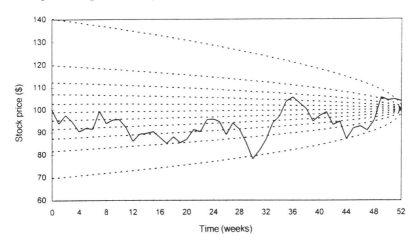

Long volatility profit

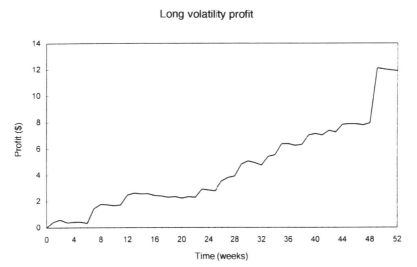

Figure 4.13   Simulation No. 1 Actual volatility = 30%

times and each time the stock hedge is adjusted. Each time the hedge is adjusted a small profit is locked in. The lower panel shows the gradual build-up of the overall profit. This particular simulation shows a high profit not only because of the high volatility but also because the stock price path happened to stay in the high gamma region right up to expiry. The final surge in profit in the last five weeks is due to

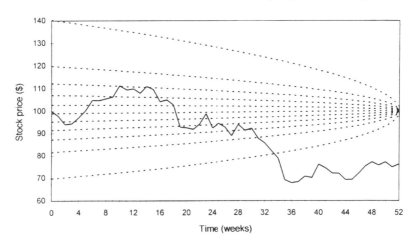

Long volatility profit

Figure 4.14 Simulation No. 2 Actual volatility = 25%

the stock price moving through 9 of the 11 contours. In the last five weeks the portfolio was rehedged nine times.

Figure 4.14 shows the situation when the underlying volatility experienced is 25%. This is higher than that paid for and so a profit still occurs. This series has a negative drift and after 34 weeks the stock price is so low that the delta of the option would be zero. After the 34th week point the stock path never re-enters the useful zone and so no further profits are made.

Figure 4.15 shows the situation when the underlying volatility experienced is very low at 5%. This series has a positive trend and so the rehedging activity would have been all one way—selling stock all the

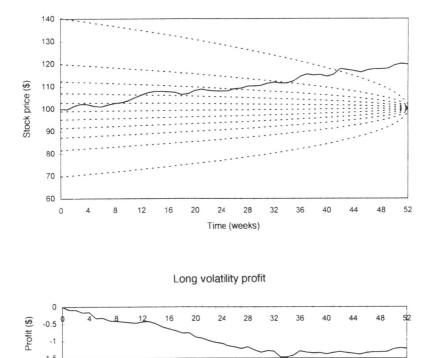

Figure 4.15   Simulation No. 1 Actual volatility = 5%

way up. As with Figure 4.14 the stock path wanders into the non-useful zone and never returns. This then illustrates the situation when one experiences less volatility than one paid for. The total overall loss in the third simulation is $1.45 or $145 per option contract.

4.11   VEGA EFFECTS ON DELTA AND GAMMA

In all of the above we assumed that the volatility parameter used by market practitioners remained fixed throughout the life of the option. This is often not the case. Halfway through the life of an option the market participants may suddenly perceive that the future volatility is going to fall. In such a situation, other things being equal, the option price will ride on a lower curve. This was illustrated in Figure 4.6 and close inspection of the curves will show that the changes in the delta and the gamma due to volatility movements is almost identical to that due to time.

Falling volatilities will have a similar effect to that of time passing, i.e.:

1. A gradually falling option price level with more pronounced falls near-the-money.
2. Far out-of-the-money options will have decreasing deltas and decreasing gammas.
3. Deep on-the-money options will have increasing deltas and decreasing gammas.
4. Near-the-money options will have increasing gammas.

This can be good or bad news for the long volatility player. Whatever the situation, the portfolio will suffer an immediate mark to market loss due to the option price fall. However, if the stock price is near the exercise price, then the increase in gamma can actually mean that there is much more scope for rehedging than before. Although there may be an initial loss this can be more than offset by the increased chance of future rehedging activity. We have talked about a drop in volatility. What happens if there is a sudden increase in volatility?

With **increasing volatilities** the effects are the reverse, i.e.:

1. A gradually increasing option price level with more pronounced increases near-the-money.
2. Far out-of-the-money options will have increasing deltas and increasing gammas.
3. Deep in-the-money options will have decreasing deltas and increasing gammas.
4. Near-the-money options will have decreasing gammas.

Understanding the complexities of the effects of the stock price, the time to expiry and the volatility on the option price, the delta and the gamma is essential in managing a volatility strategy. The simple long volatility strategy will make a profit in the right circumstances and will make a loss in the wrong circumstances. The right circumstances are buying relatively low implied volatility options and subsequently experiencing relatively high volatility. This can mean buying volatility at 25% and experiencing 35% or buying at 5% and experiencing 15%. The wrong circumstances are buying what one thought was relatively low volatility and actually experiencing even lower volatility. With any trading strategy it is useful to look at what is the most one can make or lose. We need to examine the worst and best case scenarios.

4.12   WORST CASE SCENARIO

The strategy needs volatility to make a profit and the worst case scenario is that in which there is no volatility at all. There are a number of ways a price series can have zero volatility.

The simplest case is that of the stock price staying completely constant through to expiry. As expiry approaches the hedge will be altered but all transactions will involve stock at the one constant price and on expiry the stock hedge will be completely unwound at the same constant price. In this situation the only loss to the strategy will be the time value of the option. Figure 4.16 shows the losses (type 1) suffered under this type of zero volatility.

A second type of zero volatility (type 2), that in fact can cause higher losses, is that in which the stock price moves in a gradual and orderly fashion towards the exercise price, finishing exactly at the exercise price on the expiry date. The option will thus always expire worthless, resulting in the total loss of the initial option value. If the option was initially in-the-money then these losses will be slightly offset by the profits caused by the short stock position. If the option is initially out-of-the-money then these losses will be added to by the

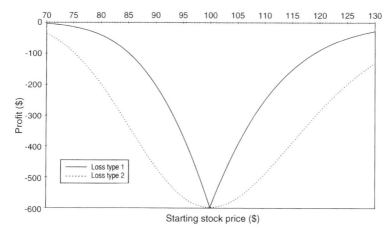

Figure 4.16   Worst case scenarios for long volatility strategy

short stock position. Figure 4.16 gives the detailed results for a number of different situations.

As an illustration we work through the calculations with the stock price starting at $120 and the option price at $20.89. At these levels the delta is 0.9 and so a neutral portfolio will contain one option and short 90 units of stock. We assume that the stock price gradually falls to $100 by expiry. Other things being equal, falling stock prices will usually have the effect of reducing the delta. However, we know from section 4.8 that, other things being equal, the delta of in-the-money options increases as expiry approaches. For simplicity and to make the arithmetic easier let us assume that the effects of a falling stock price and time passing cancel out and that the delta remains constant at 0.9. This means that there will be no additional rehedging profits and that on expiry we buy back all 90 stock units at $100. The stock hedge has provided a revenue of $90 \times (120 - 100) = \$1,800$ and this offsets the loss of $20.89 \times 100 = \$2,089$ on the option. The overall loss is thus $289 which is $200 more than the time value in the original option. It should be noted that these are very contrived situations and that it is possible to concoct situations where the losses are a little (but not much) greater. The important point to note is that it is possible to calculate beforehand what the likely maximum losses are. The long volatility strategy has a **limited loss** and the worst possible scenario is that of losing all of the initial option value plus some limited losses on the short hedge.

Before we leave the discussion of the worst case scenario it is interesting to look again at why the second of the two scenario results above are worst case. The outcomes are so bad because (1) the entire option value is lost and (2) there are no rehedging profits. In order for there to be absolutely no rehedging, the delta of the option must remain constant as time passes. We considered a very contrived situation in which time passing and the stock price moving had opposite effects on the delta, resulting in the delta remaining unchanged. This situation is in fact the one also depicted in Figure 4.12—the delta contour diagram. We see now that it is possible to view the fixed delta contour diagram in a different way. If, during the life of the option, the stock price describes one of the fixed delta contours then there will be no opportunity for rehedging and the resultant loss will correspond to one of the worst case scenarios given in Figure 4.16. It is clear that the stock price has to move in a very particular way for a worse case outcome to result.

4.13 BEST CASE SCENARIOS

There are many best case scenarios, the most obvious one being that immediately after implementation of the trade, the stock price swings violently up and down around the point of maximum gamma (near-the-money). There are, however, two other interesting extreme situations in which very large profits can be made. To illustrate these scenarios consider again the initial delta neutral portfolio outlined in Table 4.2. The stock price is at $99, the option price is at $5.46 and the hedge ratio (delta) is 0.5. The portfolio contains one long call option and short 50 shares. We know that if the stock price moves away from $99, either way, profits appear.

A Market Crash

Say immediately after instigation, the stock price suddenly collapses $60 to $39. At this level the option will be so far out-of-the-money as to be worthless and so one will have lost all of the $546 of option value. If we assume that the rate of the fall was so great that there was no time to rehedge, the profit on the 50 units of short stock would be = 50 × 60 = $3,000 resulting in a net profit of 3,000 − 546 = $2,454. If the price had fallen more than $60 the profit would have been even greater. It is easy to see how individuals executing this strategy made huge profits in the 1987 stock market crash.

A Market Ramp

Say the reverse situation occurs. Immediately after instigation, the stock price suddenly rises $60 to $159. At this level the option will be so deep in-the-money that it will be priced at intrinsic value, i.e. $59 giving a profit of 100 × (59 − 5.64) = $5,336. The short stock loss will be = 50 × 60 = $3,000 and so the net profit will be 5,336 − 3,000 = $2,336. If the price rise had been more than $60 then the profit would have been even greater.

From time to time these situations do occur. Over the years there have been a number of very large price falls and also many instances of take-over bids causing almost instantaneous price hikes. The long volatility strategy always benefits from such large price changes. The profit produced depends on the severity of the price moves. In market crashes stock prices can go no lower than zero and so it is possible to calculate maximum profit ($4,404 in the above example). There is theoretically no upper limit on a stock price and so it is not possible to put an upper limit on the profit. The long volatility play therefore has an **unlimited profit potential** and this together with the **limited loss** feature makes it a very attractive strategy.

5
The Short Volatility Trade

In Chapter 4 we outlined the simplest form of the long volatility trade; that of having a long call option and an opposing short in the underlying stock. The idea behind the strategy is to capitalise on future volatility in the stock price. If the option is cheap enough and/or the future volatility is high enough, a profit results. The strategy generates profits by buying stock low and selling high and the overall trade produces a net positive profit if these rehedging gains exceed the time decay losses. To make a positive profit the circumstances have to be right. Sometimes one may take the view that the options are very expensive and/or the stock volatility is going to fall. Paying up for expensive option premiums and witnessing little or no market movement may produce losses. If the options are expensive enough one may choose to take the opposite position and **sell volatility**. The short volatility strategy is exactly the opposite of the long volatility strategy in every respect and obviously can, in the right circumstances, produce profits. The basic strategy involves selling call options short and hedging with a long position in the stock. Before we go on to discuss the trade in detail we should consider the situation of an individual holding a short call option position.

5.1 THE SHORT CALL OPTION

Consider again the definition of a call option given in Chapter 3. A call option gives the holder the right but not the obligation to buy a given quantity of stock (100 shares) at a given price (the exercise price) on or before a given date (the expiry date). Call options are not like stock in that they are not issued by a corporation but are **sold short** or **written** by other market participants. Every time someone buys an exchange traded stock call option someone must sell one. For every long position there is a short position. What does it feel like being short a call option? The key phrase in the definition of the option is "the right but not the obligation". The holder (i.e. the party who bought the option) has the right but not the obligation. The individual who is long the option can choose, on or before expiry, if he wants to take up the stock or not. This crucial aspect of a call option gives rise to the special kinked expiry price profile shown in Figure 3.1.

Imagine now the situation of being short such a call option (exercise price = \$100). If you are short this instrument you have given someone else (the holder) the option to choose between calling stock from you at \$100 or not. You have no say in the decision but will have an idea as to what the holder will do. If the stock price is above \$100 on expiry he will issue a call notice and you have to deliver stock in return for payment of \$100 per share. If you do not already own stock you have to go into the market and buy some. If the price has risen significantly this can involve large losses. Say the stock price on expiry is \$120, then the call notice will entail you buying stock at \$120 and selling on to the option holder at \$100, a loss of \$20 per share. Since there is no upper limit to share prices one can see that shorting call options can be a very dangerous activity. In practice one does not usually need to go to the bother of buying the stock; it is often easier to just buy back the short option and suffer the same loss. But what if the stock price is below \$100 on expiry? Obviously the holder would choose not to exercise his right to buy stock at \$100 since it is cheaper in the market. In this situation, the holder would let the option expire worthless. In this situation the individual who shorted the option would be essentially buying it back at zero. This is the best outcome for **naked writers** of call options. The term "naked" here refers to short call positions that are not hedged in any way. Naked sellers take in option premiums and hope that worthless expiry results. Recall the one year call option referred to throughout Chapters 3 and 4. With the stock price at \$99 and one year to go, the option is priced at \$5.46. A naked call writer selling one option would receive \$546. If the instrument expires out-of-the-money and worthless he would be essentially buying the option back at \$0 and have made a profit of \$546. This is the most the seller can make and that is the situation of all option sellers; the very best they can do is to keep the initial option premium and there is no limit on the very worse that can happen.

Option sellers and option buyers are always in opposite situations. Every dollar made by one party is a dollar lost by the other. Option sellers have a limited profit potential and an unlimited loss potential whereas option buyers have a limited loss potential and an unlimited profit potential. Expiring profit and loss profiles are therefore also opposite but in a graphical sense. Opposite in a graphical sense here means all diagrams of short option positions are mirror images of long option positions. Figure 5.1 gives the expiring "value" of the long and short call option in question.

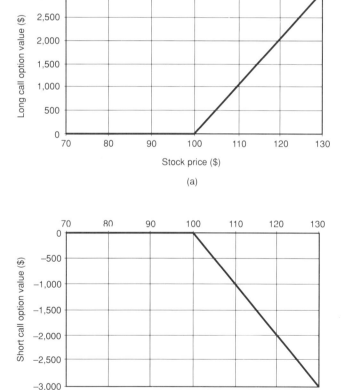

Figure 5.1 Value of (a) a long call option on expiry and (b) a short call option on expiry

Figure 5.1(a) shows the value of the long call option as either positive or zero and Figure 5.1(b) the short call option as negative or zero. With the stock price at $120 the long option is worth $20 per share or $2,000 and this is the sum realised by the holder on closing out (i.e. selling) his long position. At this stock price the short option is shown as worth − $2,000 meaning that this is the sum the writer has to pay up to close out (i.e. buy back) his short position. The negative sign is used to illustrate the fact that at this stock price the short position is in debt to the tune of − $2,000. At higher stock prices the debt to the short position increases and this is clearly illustrated by the negatively sloping line. Above the exercise price the expiring profile has a slope of − $100. Every increase in $1 causes a loss of $100 to the option seller. Above the exercise price the stock exposure is short 100 units.

5.2 SENSITIVITIES OF THE SHORT CALL OPTION POSITION

The situation of the individual short of a call option prior to expiry is the opposite in every sense to that of the individual long of a call option and so the sensitivities such as delta, gamma, theta and vega are very easy to derive. Prior to expiry, the price (and value) profile of a short call option is curved but in the opposite sense. The negative values of the expiring short call option shown in Figure 5.1 represent the total sum of money required to unwind the position, i.e. represent the degree of debt the position is in. Figure 5.1 shows the total option **values** and as with other instruments, the option **prices** that are expressed on a per share basis are simply the values divided by 100. It is also possible to represent the option prices prior to expiry on a per share basis as negative numbers. Figure 5.2 shows the price, delta and gamma profile of a portfolio short of the one-year call option. In the market-place a call option has a real and positive price, but these graphical representations using negative numbers are just to illustrate the changes in value to the individual short an option. If the price of a short option changes from − $1.00 per share to − $2.00 per share, the position has lost $1.00 per share. If the price changes from − $20.00 per share to − $18.00 per share, the position has made $2.00 per share.

When the underlying stock price is $99 the slope of the curve (the delta) is − 0.5 and so being short one call option here is equivalent to

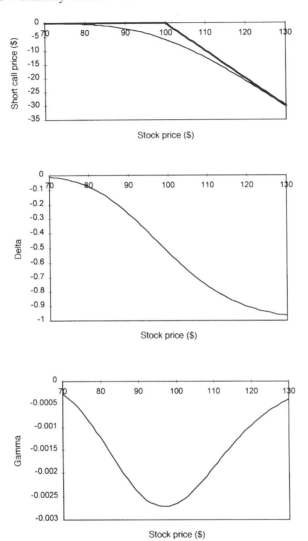

Figure 5.2   Short option price—delta—gamma

being exposed to 50 short units of stock. Note that as the underlying stock price rises the slope of the price profile becomes more and more negative. At very high stock prices the slope approaches the limiting value of -1.0 and so being short a deep in-the-money call option would feel like being short 100 units of stock.

Other things being equal, time passing causes options to fall in price. Being short an instrument that is falling in price is beneficial.

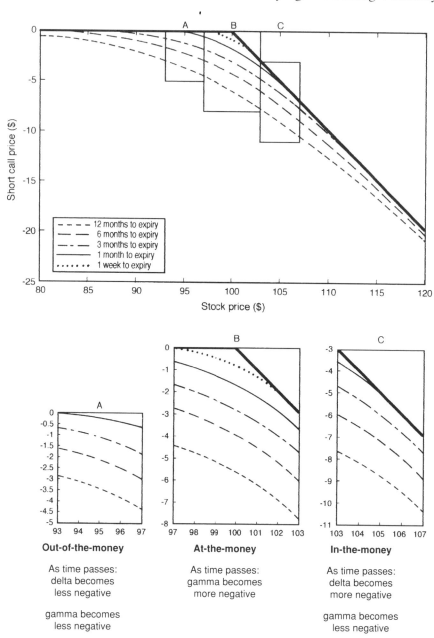

Figure 5.3   Time decay effects on short call option position

Time decay (theta) is a plus for short option positions and Figure 5.3 shows how time passing affects the option price and the delta at various stock prices. Near-the-money options suffer the most time decay and far-out-of-the-money and deep-in-the-money options suffer the least. So the situation is exactly the reverse of the long option player. Shorting at-the-money options (if the stock price stays constant) provides the most profit.

The way in which the delta changes over time is also the reverse of that of the long option position. The deltas of in-the-money options decrease, i.e. become more and more negative as time passes and so in the limit all in-the-money options eventually behave as if the position is short 100 units of stock. The deltas of out-of-the-money options increase, i.e. become less and less negative as time passes and so in the limit all out-of-the-money options have zero stock exposure.

The gamma or curvature of a short call option position is negative or zero. The price profile is curved downwards and as the underlying price increases the gamma is a measure of the rate of change of this downward-sloping profile. Near-the-money the rate at which the slope is decreasing is maximum and so at this point the gamma is most negative. In-the-money and out-of-the-money the rate at which the slope changes is small and at these extremes the gamma is correspondingly small or zero.

The effects of volatility on the sensitivities of a short call position are similarly the opposite to those on a long call position and the details are left as an exercise for the reader.

5.3 THE SIMPLE SHORT VOLATILITY TRADE

Selling expensive options can produce significant returns and the short volatility player sells options in the hope that the premium he receives more than covers any future price movements. Simply selling naked call options is very risky. Shorting call options is equivalent to establishing a short position in the underlying shares and if the market price rises, large losses can result. As with the long volatility play it is assumed that the individual has no view on the direction of the underlying and so the classic short volatility portfolio will have short call options perfectly hedged with a long stock position. Let us return to the one-year call option. With the stock price at $99 and the option price at $5.46 the delta will be -0.50. The initial portfolio will comprise one short call option and long 50 units of stock. We are at point B in Figure 5.4 which together with Table 5.1 shows the profit and loss to the portfolio, assuming for simplicity, that there is no time decay.

We now consider what happens to the portfolio under two scenarios. If the stock price rises, a loss is suffered on the short call and a profit is enjoyed on the long stock. If the stock price falls, a profit is enjoyed

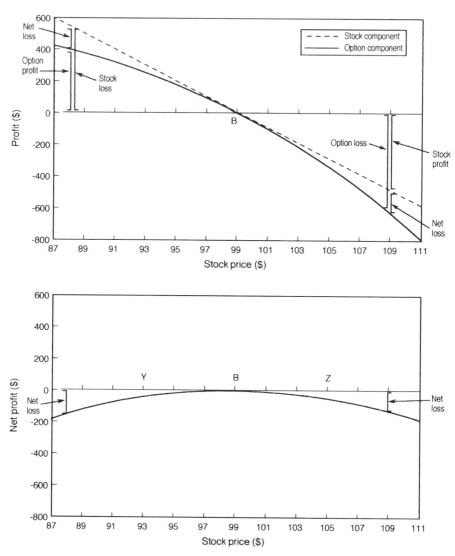

Figure 5.4 The short volatility trade

Table 5.1 The simple short volatility trade with no time decay

Stock price	Stock component (long 50 shares)		+	Option component (short one contract)		=	Short volatility portfolio
	Value of shares = 50 × price	Change in value of position from start point		Option price	Value of option contract = −100 × price	Change in value of option contract from start point	Net profit of total portfolio
93.0	4,650	−300		2.93	−293	+253	−47
94.0	4,700	−250		3.28	−328	+218	−32
95.0	4,750	−200		3.67	−367	+179	−21
96.0	4,800	−150		4.07	−407	+139	−11
97.0	4,850	−100		4.51	−451	+95	−5
98.0	4,900	−50		4.97	−497	+49	−1
98.9	4,945	−5		5.41	−541	+5	0
99.0	**4,950**	**0**		**5.46**	**−546**	**0**	**0**
99.1	4,955	+5		5.51	−551	−5	0
100.0	5,000	+50		5.98	−598	−52	−2
101.0	5,050	+100		6.52	−652	−106	−6
102.0	5,100	+150		7.09	−709	−163	−13
103.0	5,150	+200		7.69	−769	−223	−23
104.0	5,200	+250		8.30	−830	−284	−34
105.0	5,250	+300		8.95	−895	−349	−49

on the short call and a loss is suffered on the long stock. In Figure 5.4 we have shown the stock profit and loss line displayed as a negative sloping line but of course in reality it is positive. Illustrated this way it is easy to see that the net profit and loss to the hedged portfolio will be the difference between the two value profiles and this is given separately in the lower panel.

Small Stock Price Moves

If the stock price rise is small, the option losses are almost completely cancelled by the profit on the long stock. If the stock price fall is small the option profits are almost completely cancelled by the losses on the long stock. The portfolio is perfectly hedged and remains so with small stock price moves.

Large Stock Price Moves

If the stock price rises significantly, the option component always loses more than is made by the stock component. If the stock price falls significantly, the losses on the stock component always exceed the profits on the option component. The bigger the move, up or down, the bigger the losses. After putting on this position one would hope for little or no stock price movement until expiry and this is why the strategy is called the short volatility trade. The reason the portfolio always produces losses whatever the direction of the underlying is again due to the curvature of the option price. In the short volatility portfolio the curvature of the option is the opposite of that in the long volatility portfolio.

Rehedging the Short Volatility Portfolio

At point B, the portfolio is perfectly hedged. The exposure of the long 50 units of stock are completely cancelled by the one short call option with a delta of -0.5. Say the stock price increases to \$105, i.e. point Z in Figure 5.4. At Z, the portfolio has an unrealised loss of \$49 and this loss will obviously increase if the underlying price keeps increasing. At Z, the delta of the option is now -0.66 and so to be strictly market neutral we should buy an additional 16 shares to bring the total long stock position up to 66. Buying the additional shares re-establishes a delta neutral position. If the underlying price continues to increase there will still be losses but they will be smaller than those suffered if the additional shares were not purchased.

Say that immediately after buying the extra 16 shares at $105, the underlying price begins to fall all the way back to B at $99. At B, the portfolio is unbalanced again with the delta at -0.50 and so we must sell the 16 shares at $99 locking in a loss of $16 \times (105 - 99) = \$96$. If the price continues to fall we must readjust the option by selling more shares at an even lower price. At $93 (point Y) the delta is only -0.34 and so 50 shares is too heavy a hedge; the correct quantity is 34. Accordingly we would sell 16 shares at $93. If the price turns around again, then to keep market neutral we would have to start buying shares all the way up. At Z the delta is again -0.50 and so one must buy 16 shares at $99, locking in a loss of $16 \times (99 - 93) = \$96$. So being short of volatility and suffering significant price moves always involves **selling low and buying high**—the exact opposite of being long of volatility. The rehedging process, although always re-establishing a neutral position, locks in losses. Selling low and buying high is a direct result of the fact that the delta of the option position moves in the opposite direction to that of the underlying or put more simply the position has **negative gamma**. The position is short gamma and this expression is sometimes used instead of short volatility.

So why rehedge? Consider the situation of the stock price moving from B to Z to B to Y to B, etc. as in Chapter 4. Rehedging at Z, B, Y, B ... etc. would involve buying stock at $105 selling at $99, selling more at $93 only to buy back at $99 and so on. Each round trip would essentially lock in a loss of $192. If the stock price always returned to B after a $6 swing to Z or Y and we did not rehedge then no losses would occur. And that is the dilemma of the short volatility player. Once the underlying stock price has moved when does one rehedge? We know that if the price moves all the way back to the starting point we should not, with hindsight, have rehedged. In a rising market it is painful buying stock knowing that you might have to sell it all again if the price falls. But if you do not buy stock on the way up the potential losses are unlimited. The same applies to falling prices. In a falling stock price situation the hedge has to be continually unwound by selling stock. If one decides to wait in the hope that the share price will rise again the potential losses can also be very large.

5.4   TIME DECAY AND VEGA EFFECTS

The description of the above strategy makes one ask the question "Why would anyone enter into a trade that produces losses whichever way a stock price moves?" The answer is that we have not told the complete story. For ease of exposition we conveniently assumed that the option price depended only on the underlying stock price. In reality, time and the market perception of volatility will affect the option price. Time is on the side of the short volatility player. Every day that passes is a day nearer to expiry and a day in which some time value will hopefully fall out of the option. Figure 5.5 shows the much more realistic situation of including the passing of time.

Vega effects are also important. Most market participants use the same model or variations of the same model to price options and the single most important parameter defining relative option value is the implied volatility. An option with an implied volatility of 10% is cheaper than one with an implied volatility of 15%. It may be that the simple trade outlined above is instigated because it is believed that the option implied volatility of 15% is too high for the market in question and that eventually the rest of the market will mark the options down in price. If this were to happen, other things being equal, the option price profile will fall to a lower level resulting in a profit to this strategy. It should be noted that the reverse can also happen, i.e. that the market suddenly perceives that the implied volatilities are too cheap and without anything else happening, marks up all option prices.

Whatever the reason behind the implementation of this trade, the hedge is used to reduce or remove directional risk. Whether the trader wishes to capitalise on time decay and/or believes that the options are too expensive, the hedge is an attempt to remove the risk associated with the underlying stock price rising significantly. The trade will generate a net profit if the effects of time passing and/or volatility falling, exceed the cost of rehedging.

5.5   BEST CASE SCENARIO

The most favourable outcome for the short volatility player is that immediately after instigation of the trade, the stock price volatility collapses to zero. As mentioned in Chapter 4, there are two types of

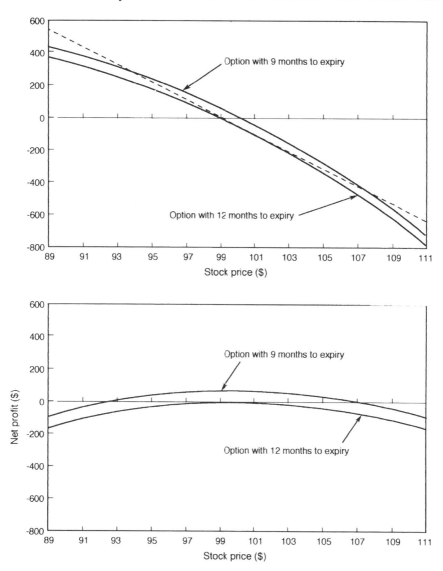

Figure 5.5 Time decay profits versus volatility losses

zero volatility worth considering and the simplest is that of the stock price staying absolutely constant until option expiry. In such a situation, the maximum profit will be equal to the loss in the option time value and this is shown for various initial stock prices in Figure 5.6 and referred to as maximum profit type 1.

The second type of zero volatility is that in which the stock price

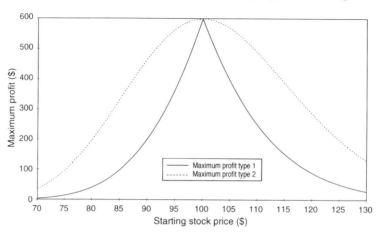

Figure 5.6 Best case scenarios for short volatility trade

moves, in an orderly fashion, towards the exercise price, ending exactly at the exercise price on expiry. If the stock price moves in such a way that the delta remains constant there will be no need to rehedge and there will be no rehedging losses. If the option is initially in-the-money, the stock price will have to gradually fall towards the exercise price in such a way that the effects of time and price on the delta will cancel out. In such a situation, the option price will fall all the way to zero resulting in a profit equal to the initial option value. This profit will be offset by the losses on the long stock hedge. If the option is initially out-of-the-money, the stock price has to move up in a gradual fashion towards the exercise price. In this situation the long stock hedge will produce a profit that is added to the option profit. The maximum profit associated with this type of stock price path is also given in Figure 5.6 and referred to as maximum profit type 2.

Consider again the fixed delta contours given in Figure 4.12. Along any given contour, the option delta is constant. These show then, the very constrained path the stock price must take in order to realise this second type of best case profit. And remember that this is a best possible scenario; this is as good as it can be. Such constrained stock price paths are very unlikely.

Figure 5.6 shows the best case scenarios for the short volatility strategy and this is simply the mirror image of Figure 4.16, the worse case scenarios for the long volatility strategy. This reinforces the opposing aspects of the two trades. The very best possible outcome for one trade is the very worst outcome for the other. The maximum profit to one trade is the maximum loss to the other.

5.6   THE WORST CASE SCENARIO

It will be no surprise to the reader that the worst case scenario for the short volatility strategy corresponds to the best case scenario for the long volatility strategy. If after implementation of the trade, the stock price swings violently up and down, the position would have to be rehedged frequently. Each up move would involve buying stock and each down move would involve selling. If this type of price behaviour continues then the losses will gradually build up and may exceed the profits caused by time decay. Two far more serious outcomes, however, correspond to one off very large price movements in one direction.

A Market Crash

Say immediately after instigation of the trade at point B, the stock price suddenly collapses $60 to $39. At this level the option will be so far out-of-the-money as to be worthless and so we will have kept all of the $546 of the initial option value. If we assume that the rate of the fall was so great that there was no time to rehedge, the loss on the 50 units of stock would be $= 50 \times 60 = \$3,000$ resulting in a net loss of $3,000 - 546 = \$2,454$. If the price had fallen more than $60 the loss would have been even greater.

A Market Ramp

This situation can be even worse. Say the reverse occurs. Immediately after instigation, the stock price suddenly rises $60 to $159. At this level the option will be so deep-in-the-money that it will be priced at intrinsic value, i.e. $59 producing a loss of $100 \times (59 - 5.64) = \$5,336$. The long stock profit will be $50 \times 60 = \$3,000$ and so the net loss will be $5,336 - 3,000 = \$2,336$. If the price rise had been more than $60 then the loss would have been even greater. In theory there is no upper limit on a stock price and so the potential losses are un-limited.

The short volatility play is therefore a strategy in which we can calculate beforehand what the maximum possible profit is but not the extent of the losses. The strategy has a **limited profit potential and an unlimited loss potential** and so is one that should be used with great caution.

5.7 LONG VOLATILITY VERSUS SHORT VOLATILITY AND MORE SIMULATIONS

One can think of all of the option market participants in terms of being either in a long volatility or a short volatility position. It is certainly true that for every long option position there is a corresponding short option position. However, the entire world is not necessarily concerned with being delta neutral. Many individuals long of call options may be speculating on a significant rise in the price of the underlying stock and many others short of call options may be using them in conjunction with long underlying stock positions. It is interesting, just as an exercise, to consider that all the open option positions are being held by two groups of individuals—those holding a delta neutral long volatility portfolio and those holding a delta neutral short volatility portfolio. If both groups agree on the same pricing model then they will have exactly opposite positions. With one year to go and the stock price at $99 (point B in Figure 5.4), one group will be long the call options and short 50 stock units per option and the other group will be short the same options and long the same quantity of stock. One party obviously believes that the option is cheap and the other that it is expensive. Time will tell who is right.

If the stock price rises to point Z, both portfolios become unbalanced but in opposite senses. The long volatility player becomes long of the market and the short volatility player becomes short. For the sake of simplicity let us assume that they both have the same rehedging strategy. At Z one party will sell 16 shares and the other will buy 16 shares. We can think of the two individuals as swapping the shares at the new, higher price of $105. As time passes and the stock price rises and falls, stock will be swapped back and forth between the two players. Each time a transaction takes place, one party will make a profit and the other will lose. Each day that passes will cause one party to lose through time decay and the other to profit. By expiry, the profits (losses) to one party will exactly match the losses (profits) to the other. So who will win and who will lose? That depends on the actual stock volatility experienced between inception and expiry. In the above example the initial price of $5.46 implied a volatility of 15%. If the subsequent volatility actually experienced is higher than 15% then the long volatility player will win over the short volatility player. If the actual volatility experienced is lower then the reverse occurs. If the actual volatility experienced is exactly 15% then both parties will break even since both entered the market at what,

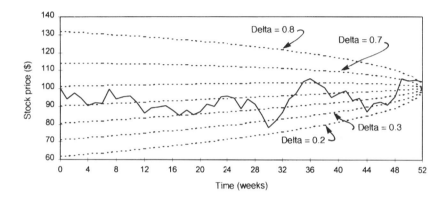

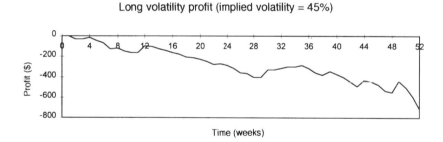

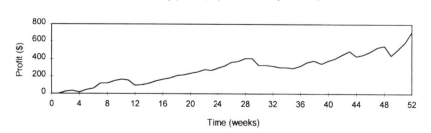

Figure 5.7   Simulation No. 1 Actual volatility = 30%

with hindsight, turned out to be the correct fair price.

This means that one can refer back to the simulations displayed in Figures 4.13–4.16 and look at them in a different light. In each figure, the upper panel shows the simulated stock price path overlaying the delta contours. Recall that in these simulations, the trading rule was that each time the delta changed by 0.10 units, rehedging occurred. So each time the stock path crosses a contour line a trade occurs. We can

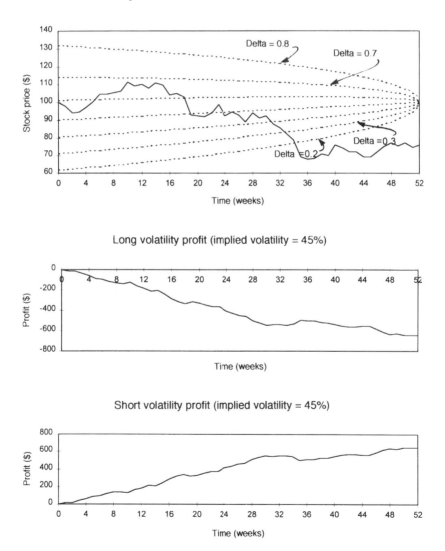

Figure 5.8 Simulation No. 2 Actual volatility = 25%

use the same simulated stock prices to demonstrate the short volatility trade. If we consider the above example in which the world consists of just the two players, then each time a contour is crossed, the two parties swap stock. The profit to one player is a loss to the other and so the profit to the short volatility trade is the mirror image of the

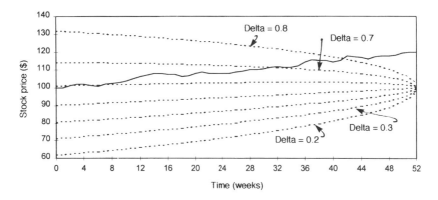

Long volatility profit (implied volatility = 45%)

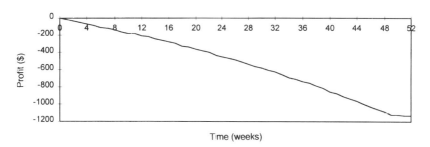

Short volatility profit (implied volatility = 45%)

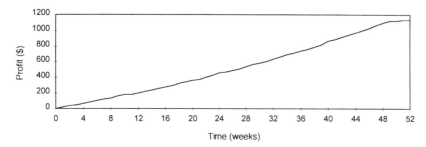

Figure 5.9 Simulation No. 3 Actual volatility = 5%

profit given in the lower panels. Price paths shown in Figures 4.13 and Figure 4.14 therefore produce short volatility losses and that shown in Figure 4.16 a profit. Recall that in all three examples the initial option implied volatility was at the relatively low value of 15%. Figures 5.7–5.9 show the profits generated by exactly the same price series but with the initial option being priced much more expensively at $17.22 with an implied volatility of 45%.

Note that the delta contours in Figures 5.7–5.9 differ slightly from those in Figures 4.13–4.16 and this is because in the later examples we have assumed that the option is priced at all times as though the underlying volatility is going to be 45% not 15%. This is a further problem for the volatility player. In order to be strictly market neutral we need an accurate estimate of the delta. If we use different volatilities in the model, not only do we get different prices, but we also get different deltas. With one year to expiry and the stock price at $99, a volatility input of 15% gives a delta of 0.50 whereas a volatility input of 45% gives a delta of 0.58. Which is the correct one? We return to this question in Chapter 7.

6
Using Put Options in Volatility Trades

The long and short volatility trades described in Chapters 4 and 5 used combinations of call options and stock. In almost every exchange traded options market in the world, for every call option there is a put option. Put options can be used in volatility trades just as easily as call options. They have not been mentioned until now in order to keep the descriptions straightforward. In this chapter we introduce the use of put options and show that, to the volatility trader, they are indistinguishable from call options. We show that the price and price sensitivities of put options can be derived directly from those of call options. The prices of puts and calls are inextricably linked. If the price of one instrument becomes disconnected from the price of the other we will show how risk-free arbitrage profits can be generated irrespective of volatility considerations.

6.1   THE PUT OPTION

There are put options on commodities, currencies, stock indexes, futures and interest rates but, as with call options, for simplicity throughout this book we will refer to put options on stocks.

Definition   A stock put option gives the right but not the obligation to **sell** a given quantity of stock at a given price on or before a given date.

The given quantity is fixed and is usually either 100 or 1,000. The given price is known as the exercise price or strike price and the given date is known as the expiry date.

In Chapter 3 we considered as an example a three-month IBM stock call option with an exercise price of $100. There will be a put option for every call option and so we will use the three-month $100 strike put option as an example and leave the issue of what the option cost until later. Consider the situation of the holder (i.e. the individual long of the put) three months hence on the expiry date. The holder must decide what to do.

1. He can exercise his option and elect to sell IBM stock at the exercise price of $100. If the market price of IBM shares are lower than $100 he would choose this option. If the stock price were say $94 he could buy 100 shares in the market and exercise his put option, forcing the other party to pay him the higher price of $100 per share. In exercising his option he has "put" stock on to someone else and made a profit of 100 − 94 = $6 per share or 6 × 100 = $600 per option contract. If the market price was even lower than $94, then the profit would be even higher.
2. He can choose not to exercise. If the stock is trading at $104 in the market then it clearly does not make sense to exercise his right to sell at $100. If he wanted to sell the stock he could sell it at a much better price in the market. In this situation he would let the option expire. He would choose this route if the stock price in the market were anything more than the exercise price of $100. In this situation the option would not have any final value at all and the put would expire worthless.

Table 6.1 and Figure 6.1 give the final value of the put option for various stock prices. One can see the attraction of puts to speculators taking a negative view on the stock market. The more the stock price falls, the higher the final put value. On first introduction it is easy to get confused about the purchase of put options. When one buys a put option one is **buying** the right to **sell** something. It is the two conflicting aspects of the previous sentence that sometimes cause confusion— one buys to sell. It is easier sometimes to think of a put option as a contract that gives you a get-out clause. The put gives you the ability, if you so choose, to get rid of your stock holdings at a prearranged price. The put is like an insurance contract and the put price can be thought of as simply the cost of insurance.

In point 1 above we calculated the expiring put value by assuming that the holder would go into the market, buy stock at $94, exercise

Table 6.1 Expiring value of put option with exercise price = $100

Stock price on expiry ($)	Value of put option on expiry ($)
90	10 × 100 = 1,000
92	8 × 100 = 800
94	6 × 100 = 600
96	4 × 100 = 400
98	2 × 100 = 200
100	0
102	0
104	0
106	0
108	0
110	0

his $100 strike option, pass on the stock and receive $100 per share. In practice this is often not necessary. As with calls, the put could be sold at its intrinsic price of $6, saving all the bother and costs associated with the share transactions.

We see that the expiring put option value profile (Figure 6.1) is a vertical mirror image of that of an expiring call option value profile given in Figure 3.1 and this characteristic leads on to some very simple relationships between the two instruments. Both have a discontinuity or kink at $100, both increase in value in one direction and both have

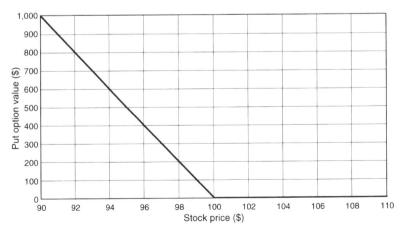

Figure 6.1 Put option value on expiry (exercise price = $100)

zero value in the other direction. Above the exercise price the put value line is horizontal and hence has stock exposure is zero. Below the exercise price the put value increases $100 for every $1 drop in stock price and so the stock exposure is short 100 units.

Put option terminology is similar to that of call options. The only difference is that a put option whose exercise price is above the current stock price is called in-the-money and one whose exercise price is below the current stock price is called out-of-the-money. So a $100 strike put option priced at $5 is in-the-money if the stock price is $97. In this example the intrinsic value of the put is $3 and the time value is $2. If an individual buys this put at $5 outright he is speculating that the stock price will fall. If the stock price falls to $75 by expiry then the put will be priced at $25. This is the attraction to the speculator. In this example the stock price fell only 25% whereas the put increased 400%.

6.2 PUT PRICE SENSITIVITIES PRIOR TO EXPIRY

Recall the discussion in Chapter 3 in which the shape of the call option price profile prior to expiry was derived. We first discussed the meaning of fair value. The fair value of the call was defined to be the long-run average of the final expiring option values. We considered an individual repeatably playing a game of chance in which he always bought the same call. Since the expiring call values are known with certainty for each particular stock price, all that was required was a suitable distribution. Using a very naïve distribution that assumed each of a discrete number of different prices was equally likely, one arrived at a nonlinear or curved price profile. It was shown in detail that the nonlinearity or curvature came out of the averaging process. The real reason for the curvature is that the averaging process involves varying numbers of zeros; the zeros are there because of the kink in the expiring profile. We finally introduced a much more realistic distributional assumption, that of the lognormal distribution, and stated that the resulting mathematical model, the Black and Scholes model, is now the universally accepted industry standard.

We could go through the entire process again to derive the put price profile prior to expiry but it is not really necessary. It is easy to see that the result will be very similar. The put price before expiry will also be curved and the curvature is there because of the kink on expiry. The curve will have a different aspect since this time the zeros occur at high stock prices and the non-zeros occur at low stock prices. The Black and Scholes model gives the put prices and Table 6.2 and Figure 6.2 show these and the sensitivities for a one year put with an exercise price of $100 assuming, as with the call, a volatility of 15%. For simplicity we assume that the stock pays no dividend and that interest rates are zero.

The put price profile is curved in a very similar manner to the call price profile. At extreme stock prices, the curve approaches and becomes indistinguishable from the limiting boundaries. In between extremes the price rides above the boundaries along a smooth curve. The reason for this behaviour is to do with the averaging process and the various probabilities associated with different stock prices. The slope of the price curve (the delta) is negative, indicating various degrees of negative stock exposure. Deep in-the-money puts have deltas near—1.0 and far out-of-the-money puts have deltas near zero. Recall that the gamma of an option is the rate of change of the delta with respect to the underlying stock. We note that although the deltas are negative, they become less negative (i.e. increase) as the underlying increases. So the gamma of a long put option is positive—deltas increase with increasing stock prices. Note that like the call option, the rate of increase is greatest near-the-money and least at the extremes and this can also be observed from looking directly at the price curve.

Table 6.2 Price and price sensitivities of one-year put option

Stock price ($)	Option price ($)	Option delta	Option gamma
70	30.04	−0.99	0.00268
75	25.14	−0.97	0.00650
80	20.40	−0.92	0.01227
85	15.98	−0.84	0.01884
90	12.02	−0.73	0.02427
95	8.67	−0.61	0.02703
100	5.98	−0.47	0.02654
105	3.95	−0.34	0.02339
110	2.50	−0.24	0.01879
115	1.52	−0.16	0.01393
120	0.89	−0.10	0.00964
125	0.50	−0.06	0.00628
130	0.28	−0.03	0.00387

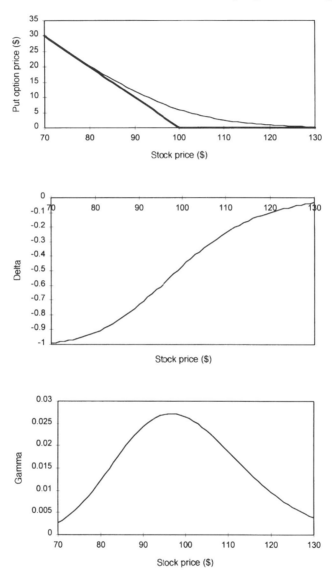

Figure 6.2 Put option price—delta—gamma

The curvature is most pronounced near-the-money and almost non-existent at the extremes.

It is no coincidence that the gammas of a long put option and a long call option are similar, they are in fact **identical**. Since the gammas of a put and call are identical, the volatility player views them as identical instruments. We return to this later on and show that with one very simple trade it is actually possible to turn a **put into a call** or vice versa.

6.3   TIME AND VEGA EFFECTS ON PUT OPTIONS

By this stage the reader should be sufficiently familiar with the way in which time and volatility affect call options as to be able to guess the effects on put options. As with call options, time passing and/or falling volatility will cause the put price curve to move nearer the kinked expiry boundary. One does not need a mathematical model to see how time passing affects the prices, deltas and gammas of a put option. By just drawing lower and lower curves the effects are obvious. Figure 6.3 shows how the prices and price sensitivities of a put option varies over time.

6.4   THE LONG VOLATILITY TRADE WITH PUT OPTIONS

Throughout this book we assume that the reader has no view on the direction of the stock price in question. Holders of unhedged puts, by definition, are short of the market and will lose (profit) if the stock price rises (falls). To hedge a put one needs to take a position in something that will have the opposite effect. To hedge a put therefore one needs to buy stock or enter into a long position. The amount will be determined by the put delta. If the underlying is at a price of $99, the one-year put is priced at $6.46 and has a delta of -0.5. (It is no coincidence that this corresponds to the price at which the one-year call option has a delta of 0.5.) The simple long volatility trade will thus have a long position in one put and a hedge of $0.5 \times 100 = 50$ units long in the underlying. Table 6.3 and Figure 6.4 give the profit and loss to the portfolio if the underlying price moves and there is no time decay.

For ease of exposition the profit and loss to the stock component is plotted in the reverse sense, so what appears below (above) the zero line as a loss is in fact a profit (loss). The net profit to the strategy appears in the final column of Table 6.3 and in the lower panel of Figure 6.4. The net profit is exactly the same as that given for the long

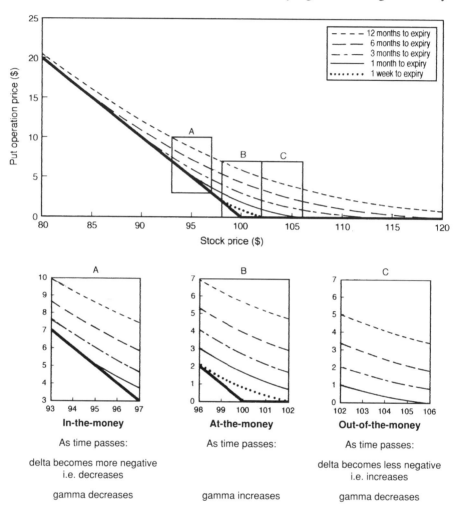

Figure 6.3 Time decay effects on long put option

volatility strategy using calls in Table 4.2 and Figure 4.2 respectively. If the stock price rises or falls the profit to the strategy using puts and calls is the same dollar for dollar.

The interesting point is that the rehedging strategy is also identical. If the underlying price rises the short stock exposure of the put decreases and since the portfolio contains 50 long units of stock the total portfolio becomes net long. In order to rehedge the trader would have to sell stock. The position at B initially is long of 50 shares, so at

Z (stock price = $105) when the delta of the put has changed to -0.34 the hedge should only be 34 shares and so 16 shares are sold. Compare this with the long volatility portfolio using a call option. At B the call is hedged with 50 short shares. At Z the delta is greater at 0.66, at which point **16 extra** shares are sold to rehedge. Both strategies involve selling sock if the underlying price rises. The difference between the two portfolios is that with puts the original hedge is long

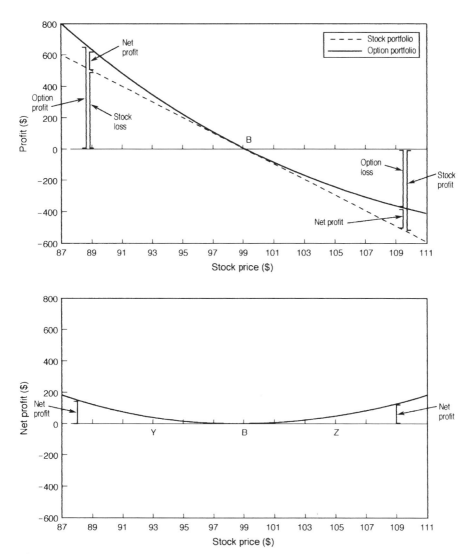

Figure 6.4 The long volatility trade with put options

Table 6.3 The simple long volatility trade using puts

	Stock component (long 50 shares)		+	Option component (long one put contract)		=	Long volatility portfolio
Stock price	Value of shares = 50 × price	Change in value of position from start point	Option price	Value of option contract = 100 × price	Change in value of option contract from start point		Net profit of total portfolio
93.0	4,650	−300	9.93	993	+347		+47
94.0	4,700	−250	9.28	928	+282		+32
95.0	4,750	−200	8.67	867	+221		+21
96.0	4,800	−150	8.07	807	+161		+11
97.0	4,850	−100	7.51	751	+105		+5
98.0	4,900	−50	6.97	697	+51		+1
98.9	4,945	−5	6.51	651	+5		0
99.0	**4,950**	**0**	**6.46**	**646**	**0**		**0**
99.1	4,955	+5	6.41	641	−5		0
100.0	5,000	+50	5.98	598	−48		+2
101.0	5,050	+100	5.52	552	−94		+6
102.0	5,100	+150	5.09	509	−137		+13
103.0	5,150	+200	4.69	469	−177		+23
104.0	5,200	+250	4.30	430	−216		+34
105.0	5,250	+300	3.95	395	−251		+49

shares and selling involves reducing the position but with calls the original hedge is short shares and selling involves increasing the position. But the net effect is the same—one sells into a rising market.

It is easy to see that the rehedging strategy is also identical if the underlying price falls—one buys stock on the way down. So the long volatility strategy using puts is identical in every way to that using calls. In volatile markets one buys low and sells high, accumulating rehedging profits. These rehedging profits are of course offset by time decay and the trade will only make a net profit if the volatility experienced over the life of the option is higher than that originally paid for—the volatility implied by the price of the option at inception.

As when using calls, the long volatility strategy using puts produces rehedging profits because of the presence of price curvature or gamma, and the basic idea underpinning the strategy is to find cheap options with high gamma. Since the gamma of a put and call are identical, the volatility player views them as identical instruments. This is the fascinating aspect of the two options. To the speculator they are completely different investment vehicles. You buy one if you think the market is going to rise and the other if you think it is going to fall. But to the volatility player they are the same. The only difference between using a call or put in a volatility strategy will be the nature of the original hedge. After instigation, the rehedging strategy will be identical and this is all due to the fact that the instruments have one thing in common; they have the same price kink on expiry.

All the aspects of the long volatility trade using calls discussed in Chapter 4 thus directly apply to the trade using puts. The effects of time decay, the effects of volatility changes, the simulated profits and the best and worst case scenarios will be identical. The only difference is that one portfolio is hedged using short shares and the other is hedged using long shares. The important point to note is that both portfolios are **long of options**.

6.5   THE EQUIVALENCE OF PUT AND CALL OPTIONS

The fact that the profit or loss to a long volatility strategy is the same whether one uses puts or calls is no coincidence. Puts and calls are very similar instruments and it is in fact possible to turn one option into another via a very simple trade. In order to see how this is done consider two fund managers, A and B, both with negative views on the direction of a particular stock price. The stock price at the start of the period under consideration is $110 and there is a one-year put and call option with an exercise price of $100. The put and call are priced at $2.50 and $12.50 respectively. The put is out-of-the-money and the call is in-the-money. Manager A takes the simple route and buys one put option paying up $250. Manager B takes a more complicated route and buys the call (paying up $1,250) and simultaneously shorts 100 units of stock at $110.

We now consider the situation of both managers if the stock price falls all the way down to $70 by the option expiry date. Manager A sells his put at the intrinsic price of $30 and receives $3,000 thus making a profit of 3,000 − 250 = **$2,750**. The call option that manager B owns obviously expires worthless, and so he loses all his $1,250 investment. However, manager B is also short 100 units of stock and he buys this back at $70 making 100 × (110 − 70) = $4,000 profit. Manager B has thus made an overall profit of 4,000 − 1,250 = **$2,750** which is exactly the same as that made by manager A. Table 6.4 and Figure 6.5 show the profits of both fund managers for various final stock prices. The net profit to both managers is identical everywhere and so the combination of call option and short stock must be identical to being long a put option. We say that the portfolio of long a call option and short stock is in fact a synthetic put option. We can write this as an equation:

$$\textbf{Long put} = \textbf{Long call} + \textbf{Short stock} \qquad (6.1)$$

or if we replace the + short stock term with the more meaningful − long stock term we have:

$$\textbf{Long put} = \textbf{Long call} - \textbf{Long stock} \qquad (6.2)$$

So by running a short stock position alongside a long call position one has essentially turned a call into a put. It is easy to see how this works graphically. The profit profile of the call option is kinked at $100. Above $100 the call option gives the holder the exposure to 100 units of long stock. If the portfolio is at the same time short 100 units of stock these two stock exposures cancel and the resultant combination has zero exposure. Below $100 the call option has no stock exposure but the portfolio is still short 100 stock units and so the resultant combination is net short 100 units. This is exactly the same expiring

Table 6.4 The expiring profits of fund managers A and B

	Fund manager A = long of put at $2.5		Fund manager B = long of call $12.5 + short 100 shares at $110			
Stock price (a)	Put price (b)	Profit on put = 100 × ((b) −2.5) (c)	Call price (d)	Profit on call = 100 × ((d) −12.5 = (e)	Profit on stock = 100 × (110 −(a)) (f)	Call + stock profit (g) = (e) + (f)
70	30	+2,750	0	−1,250	+4,000	+2,750
75	25	+2,250	0	−1,250	+3,500	+2,250
80	20	+1,750	0	−1,250	+3,000	+1,750
85	15	+1,250	0	−1,250	+2,500	+1,250
90	10	+750	0	−1,250	+2,000	+750
95	5	+250	0	−1,250	+1,500	+250
100	0	−250	0	−1,250	+1,000	−250
105	0	−250	5	−750	+500	−250
110	0	−250	10	−250	0	−250
115	0	−250	15	+250	−500	−250
120	0	−250	20	+750	−1,000	−250
125	0	−250	25	+1,250	−1,500	−250
130	0	−250	30	+1,750	−2,000	−250

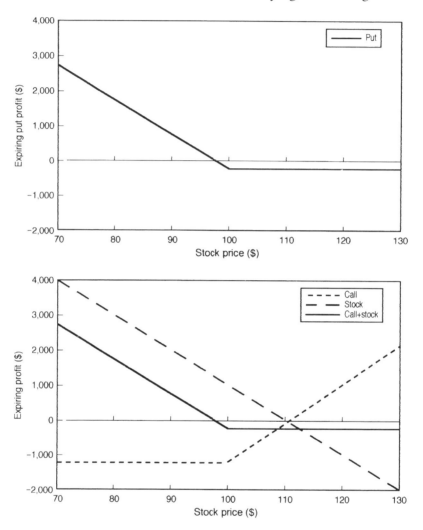

Figure 6.5 Long put versus long call + short stock

stock exposure of a long put option. Initially, in some exchange traded options markets, only call options were available. Participants wanting to take negative positions synthesised put options by buying calls and simultaneously shorting stock.

The example in Table 6.4 was chosen for simplicity. At $110 the put and call were conveniently priced at the rounded figures of $2.50 and $12.50 respectively. It is possible to show that the equivalence of a put and call option holds true whatever the original stock price and at all times, not just on expiry. If this were not the case then a risk-free arbitrage profit could be obtained irrespective of volatility or price direction. This means that the price of a put and call option with the same terms, must be inextricably linked at all times. The price of one must be a simple function of the other and in the absence of interest rates and dividends is given by the expressions

$$\textbf{Put price} = \textbf{Call price} + \textbf{Exercise price} - \textbf{Stock price} \quad (6.3)$$

or

$$\textbf{Call price} = \textbf{Put price} - \textbf{Exercise price} + \textbf{Stock price} \quad (6.4)$$

In the above example, if $12.50 is the correct price for the call option then the put price should be $12.50 + 100 - 110 = 2.50. To illustrate what can happen if this were not the case consider again the initial situation of the two fund managers above. Say manager A buys the put at $2.50 and at the same time manager B buys the call at $13.50 (not at the correct price of $12.50) and shorts 100 stock at $110. It is easy to show that whatever the final expiring stock price, the profit to manager B is always $100 less than manager A and this is because manager B paid $100 too much to synthesise the put. Either the put is too cheap at $2.50 or the call is too expensive at $13.50. If this situation existed in reality, a third individual, Mr C, could come into the market and create a risk-free arbitrage profit as follows. Mr C would buy one put as $2.50, sell short one call at $13.50 and buy 100 units of stock at $110 and wait until expiry. On expiry he would unwind the positions with a $100 risk-free profit whatever the stock price. Table 6.5 gives the details for various expiring stock prices.

If the final stock price is above $100 the loss on the short call and long put is completely cancelled by the profit on the long stock. Below $100, the loss on the long stock is completely cancelled by the profit on the long put and short call. Whatever happens, a profit of $100 results because one option was either $1 too expensive or the other was $1 too cheap. If the market price of the call is correct at $13.50 then the put price must be $= 13.50 + 100 - 110 = 3.50. Alternatively if the put is correctly priced at $2.50 then the call must be $2.50 - 100 + 110 = 12.50.

Just as one can generate a put from a call and stock, it is also possible to generate a call from a put and stock. To generate a call we need to be able to add two instruments together that on expiry will (1) have a kink at $100, (2) have zero stock exposure below $100 and (3) have 100 units long exposure above $100. The put has minus 100 units exposure below $100 and so these could be neutralised by adding 100 long stock units. This would also have the effect of introducing 100 long units above $100. So a call can be synthesised by adding 100 units of stock to a put or

$$\textbf{Long call} = \textbf{Long put} + \textbf{Long stock} \qquad (6.5)$$

Readers familiar with basic algebra will note that expression (6.5) is a simple rearrangement of expression (6.2).

So in reality we only need one type of option since we can always generate one type from the other. And the same goes for synthesising short option positions. It is left as an exercise for the reader to show the following:

$$\textbf{Short call} = \textbf{Short put} - \textbf{Long stock} \qquad (6.6)$$

$$\textbf{Short put} = \textbf{Short call} + \textbf{Long stock} \qquad (6.7)$$

One can take the subject of synthesising instruments one more stage and consider generating a synthetic stock position from put and call options. A portfolio long a put option and short the same call option is essentially short the underlying. This is demonstrated clearly by looking at the expiring option prices given in Figure 6.6. The upper panel shows the exposures of the separate components and the lower panel the exposure of a portfolio short 100 units of stock—they are identical. Above $100, the put expires worthless but the short call gives exposure of short 100 units. Below $100, the call is worthless but the long put gives exposure of short 100 units. So at all prices the combination of long put and short call is equivalent to being short 100 stock units. It is possible to show that this will be so at all stock prices and at all times, not just expiry. The identity can be expressed algebraically as

$$\textbf{Short stock} = \textbf{Long put} + \textbf{Short call} \qquad (6.8)$$

Similarly it is easy to show that a long stock position can be synthesised by a short put and a long call, i.e.

$$\textbf{Long stock} = \textbf{Short put} + \textbf{Long call} \qquad (6.9)$$

Table 6.5 The expiring profits of arbitrage fund manager C

Fund manager C = long of put at $2.5 plus short of call at $13.5 plus long 100 shares at $110

Stock price (a)	Put price (b)	Call price (c)	Profit on put = 100 × ((b) − 2.5) = (d)	Profit on call = 100 × (13.5 − (c)) = (e)	Profit on stock = 100 × ((a) − 110) = (f)	Total profit (g) = (d) + (e) + (f)
70	30	0	+2,750	+1,350	−4,000	**+100**
75	25	0	+2,250	+1,350	−3,500	**+100**
80	20	0	+1,750	+1,350	−3,000	**+100**
85	15	0	+1,250	+1,350	−2,500	**+100**
90	10	0	+750	+1,350	−2,000	**+100**
95	5	0	+250	+1,350	−1,500	**+100**
100	0	0	−250	+1,350	−1,000	**+100**
105	0	5	−250	+850	−500	**+100**
110	0	10	−250	+350	0	**+100**
115	0	15	−250	−150	+500	**+100**
120	0	20	−250	−650	+1,000	**+100**
125	0	25	−250	−1,150	+1,500	**+100**
130	0	30	−250	−1,650	+2,000	**+100**

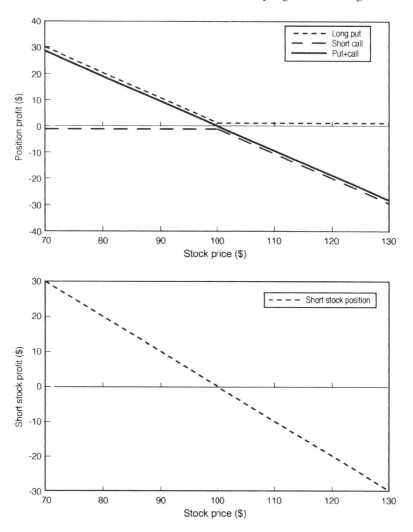

Figure 6.6 Synthesising a short stock position

So we see that stock, calls and puts are interchangeable. Any two can be used to generate the third. This link between the two types of options and the underlying stock means that the prices of all three must stay in line according to the expressions given above. If one instrument becomes too expensive relative to the other two, it is easy to synthesise an equivalent long position cheaply, short the expensive real instrument and run to expiry. Whatever the final stock price, a risk free arbitrage profit will result.

In all of the above it should be emphasised that when turning one option position into another or when synthesising stock from options, the ratio of stock to option is always one to one or more precisely 100 stock to one option exercisable into 100 shares. We have made no mention of delta. Put and call prices are linked via the zero arbitrage expressions (6.3) and (6.4). It should be no surprise that the deltas of the two options are also linked. Recall expression (6.2) again which states that at all times and at all stock prices, a long put position behaves identically to one long of a call option and short stock. Deltas are simply rates of changes of option prices with respect to the underlying stock price and so it should be clear that the rate of change of the put price will be identical to the rate of change of the price of the portfolio long of a call and short stock or

$$\text{Long put} = \text{Long call} - \text{long stock}$$

Rate of change of (long put) = Rate of change of (long call) − rate of change of (long stock)

The rate of change of a stock position with respect to the stock price is one and so

$$\textbf{Delta of put} = \textbf{Delta of call} - \textbf{1} \tag{6.10}$$

So in the long volatility example outlined above when the delta of the one year call is 0.50 the delta of the corresponding put is 0.50 − 1.00 = −0.50. At the higher stock price when the call delta is 0.66 that of the put is 0.66 − 1.00 = −0.34, etc.

We can take this argument to one final stage and derive the gamma of a put from the gamma of a call. Recall that the gamma of an option is the rate of change of delta and so we can apply this to expression (6.10) as follows:

Rate of change of (delta of put) = Rate of change of (delta of call) − Rate of change of (1)

The rate of change of 1 is of course zero so

Rate of change of (delta of put) = Rate of change of (delta of call)

or

$$\textbf{Gamma of put} = \textbf{Gamma of call} \tag{6.11}$$

This is where we started. The gammas of puts and calls with the same terms are identical and this is why volatility traders view the two instruments as the same. All of the above connections involving the prices, deltas and gammas of puts in terms of calls stems from the fact that a risk-free profit could be obtained if the links were broken.

6.6 THE SHORT VOLATILITY TRADE USING PUT OPTIONS

A long put option gives a negative stock exposure (negative delta) and so a short put option gives a long stock exposure (positive delta). Having a short position in put options is initially confusing. If you are short a put option you have given someone else (the put holder) the right but not the obligation to sell, i.e. put stock to you at a pre-arranged price (the exercise price). Being short a put option is being in a position that has the potential to turn into a long stock position. So being short a put option is very much like being long the market particularly if the stock price is falling. In Chapter 5 we dealt with short call options by simply inverting the long options characteristics. We can similarly invert the long put curves and arrive at the prices and price sensitivities of a short put position. These are given in Figures 6.7 and 6.8.

As with short calls, the negative prices represent the sum necessary to pay up to liquidate a short put position. In falling markets a short put option becomes increasingly long of the underlying. In the limit when the option is very deep in-the-money the short put position behaves exactly like a long position in 100 units of stock. To hedge a short put we obviously need to take a position that will profit from falling stock prices, i.e. a short stock position. If the delta of the short put is +0.50 then we short 50 units of stock. Table 6.6 and Figure 6.9 show the profit to the hedged portfolio for changes in stock price.

The net profit (or loss in this case) to the portfolio is exactly the same as that given in Table 5.1 and Figure 5.4, i.e. the short volatility portfolio using short call options. This should not be surprising since we know that there is a direct link between a short call and a short put. The short volatility position using puts is identical in every respect to that using calls. If the stock price falls significantly then more shares must be sold. If the stock price rises significantly then more shares must be bought. Each rehedging transaction locks in losses and these losses will be offset by the time decay profits. The worse and best case scenarios are similarly identical.

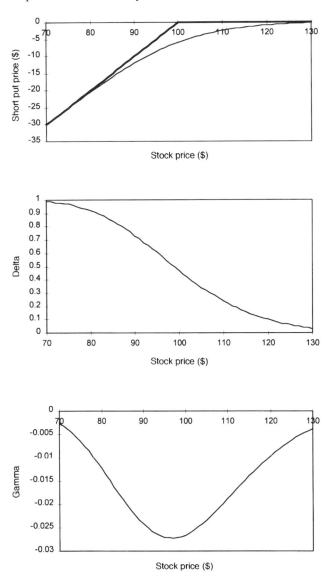

Figure 6.7   Short put option characteristics

6.7   NET OPTION POSITIONS

Up until this stage we have for simplicity talked about being either long or short volatility using just one specific call or put— the one with

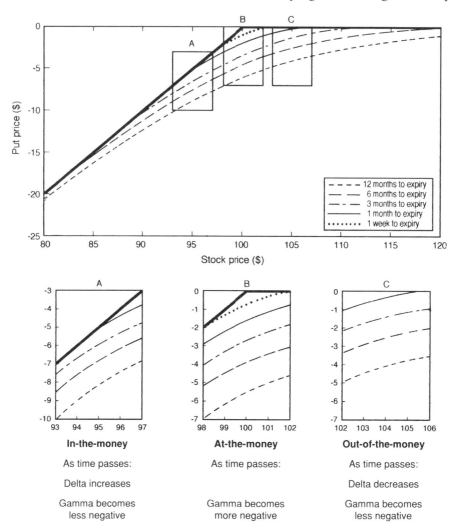

Figure 6.8 Time decay effects on short put characteristics

a year to expiry and an exercise price of $100. In reality there are many different options available, each with different expiry times and different exercise prices. A typical portfolio will have long and short positions in a variety of options and the management of such portfolios can be quite complicated and will be dealt with in more detail in Chapter 7. It is, however, possible to reduce the complexity of such portfolios by considering what the professionals call **net options positions**.

Table 6.6 The simple short volatility trade with short puts

	Stock component (short 50 shares)		+	Option component (short one put contract)		=	Short volatility portfolio
Stock price	Value of shares = 50 × price	Change in value of position start poin		Option price	Value of option contract = −100 × price	Change in value of option contract from start point	Net profit of total portfolio
93.0	4,650	+300		9.93	−993	−347	−47
94.0	4,700	+250		9.28	−928	−282	−32
95.0	4,750	+200		8.67	−867	−221	−21
96.0	4,800	+150		8.07	−807	−161	−11
97.0	4,850	+100		7.51	−751	−105	−5
98.0	4,900	+50		6.97	−697	−51	−1
98.9	4,945	+5		6.51	−651	−5	0
99.0	**4,950**	**0**		**6.46**	**−646**	**0**	**0**
99.1	4,955	−5		6.41	−641	+5	0
100.0	5,000	−50		5.98	−598	+48	−2
101.0	5,050	−100		5.52	−552	+94	−6
102.0	5,100	−150		5.09	−509	+137	−13
103.0	5,150	−200		4.69	−469	+177	−23
104.0	5,200	−250		4.30	−430	+216	−34
105.0	5,250	−300		3.95	−395	+251	−49

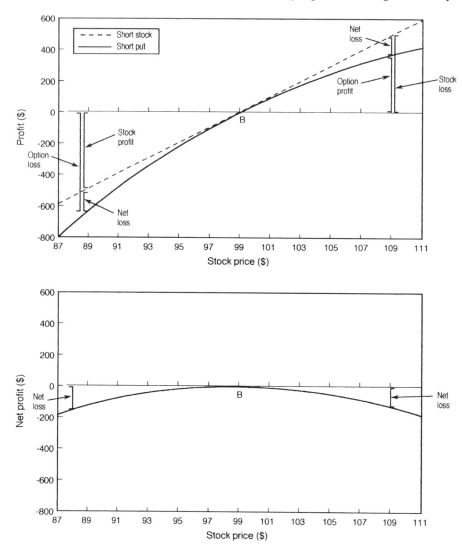

Figure 6.9 Short volatility trade with short puts

Recall the identities given by expressions (6.8) and (6.9). They state that being long one option type and simultaneously short the other option type is equivalent to having a position in the underlying stock. Being long a call and short the same put is equivalent to being long 100 units of the underlying. Being short a call and long the same put is equivalent to being short 100 units of the underlying. The volatility player is only interested in price curvature or gamma and not the direction of the price of the underlying. If the portfolio has equal and opposite positions in the same puts and calls, then these would be hedged completely out by an opposite position in the underlying and the net effect would be that the portfolio value would remain unchanged for all stock prices and at all times. The interesting point to note is that separately the three individual components would be changing in value all the time but the combination would remain constant. The overall result would be that the portfolio would be neither long nor short volatility, nor long nor short the market. The three positions of put, call and stock can be completely ignored, they can be **netted out** of the portfolio and removed from consideration. Such netting out will have the effect of reducing the apparent complexity of the overall portfolio.

The simplification of option portfolios offered by the netting out procedure can be taken one stage further. We know that the profits or losses to the long or short volatility player are the same whether using calls or puts. If the hedged portfolio is long (short) options then the participant is long (short) volatility; it does not matter whether the options are calls or puts. This means that one can talk about the portfolio being long or short options and ignore the type. To illustrate the simplicity this concept offers, consider the portfolio involving a number of one-year stock options with various exercise prices given in Table 6.7. A positive sign represents a long position and a negative sign represents a short position.

Consider each strike price in turn. The portfolio is long 20 call options of the $110 strike and so we say that the position is long 20 $110 strike options. At the $105 strike, the long 10 calls and short 10 puts are equivalent to a long position in the underlying. This long position would

Table 6.7 Net option positions

Exercise price	Call option positions	Put option positions	Net option position
110	+20	0	+20
105	+10	−10	0
100	+15	+5	+20
95	−20	−10	−30
90	+15	−20	−5
85	−30	+35	+5

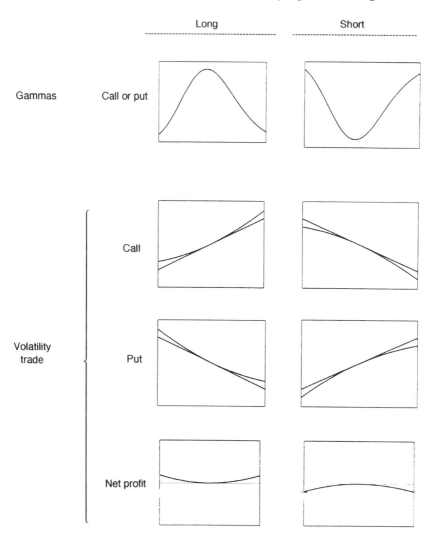

Figure 6.10   Summary of price, delta, gamma and volatility trade profits

be hedged by a short position in the stock and for simplicity is reported elsewhere. We see that the portfolio therefore has no option position at the $105 strike. The long 15 calls and long 5 puts at the $100 strike are in volatility terms equivalent to being long 20 options. Similarly at the $95 strike, the position is short 30 options. The $90 strike situation reduces to net short 5 options because one can net out 15 of the long

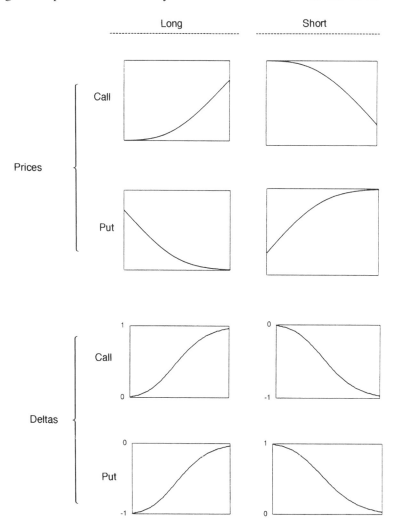

Figure 6.10 *continued*

calls with 15 of the 20 short puts leaving 5 shorts. With the $85 strike, one can net out the 30 short calls with 30 long puts leaving the portfolio long 5 puts or net long 5 options. The netting out procedure has meant that a portfolio containing 12 different positions can be viewed as a much simpler one containing only 5 positions. Such simplification is very important when considering large option portfolios.

6.8   SUMMARY OF PROFILES

Figure 6.10 gives a final summary of the price, delta, gamma and volatility trade profit profiles for the four combinations of long and short, call and put options.

7
Managing Combinations of Options

So far we have concentrated on simple portfolios containing either a long or short position in a single call or put option. In reality, for any given stock, there are usually a number of different options available. Invariably there are at least three different expiry times and at least three different exercise prices for each expiry cycle. Thus there are at least 3 (expiries) $\times$ 3 (exercise prices) $\times$ 2 (put or call) $\times$ 2 (long or short) = 36 different types of portfolio containing just one option position. It is unlikely that an options portfolio manager will concentrate on just one option and so it is necessary to look at how portfolios containing combinations of various different options behave. If there are 36 different types of portfolio containing just one option it is easy to see that there are a great number of different combinations containing two or more options. For example, there are 630 different combinations of two options, 7,140 combinations of three options and 58,905 combinations containing four options. And this is assuming that the combinations are limited to one-to-one ratios. Often managers will use different ratios such as long two calls to short three puts, etc. When this extra degree of flexibility is taken into account, the number of different possible combinations becomes enormous and managing the overall portfolio can become quite difficult.

In any given portfolio all the individual options will, to a greater or lesser extent, behave according to the industry standard Black and Scholes model. Each component will contribute positively or negatively, in varying degrees, to the overall stock exposure of the portfolio. Each component will have different degrees of time decay and different sensitivities to the market volatility. The manager of such a portfolio will need to monitor the overall effect the different components have and to be able to assess the impact of stock price moves, time passing and volatility changes. In this chapter we show how it is possible to monitor the most complex option portfolios using the simple spreadsheet software given on the disc supplied with this book. However, some of the standard option strategies involving simple combinations can be examined using straightforward graphical techniques and before we consider the more complex possibilities we look at three straightforward combinations.

7.1   COMBINATION #1: THE VERTICAL CALL SPREAD

Probably the simplest option strategy is the vertical call spread (or sometimes simply referred to as the call spread). This strategy involves buying one call option and simultaneously selling another call option with the same expiry date but a different exercise price. The example we will consider is the $100/$110 one-year call spread on the stock that we have used throughout this book. Say we buy the $100 strike option and sell the $110 strike option. If you buy the lower strike and sell the higher strike (with call options), market terminology dictates that you have bought the spread. It should be obvious that the lower strike call option will always be more expensive than the higher strike option and so the combination will have a positive price, i.e. some investment is required. Leaving aside the question of the initial call spread cost, consider the value of the combination on expiry. Table 7.1 and Figure 7.1 show the expiring values and prices of the individual components and the total spread. We use the usual notation employed for short option positions, i.e. that of negative value. A negative value represents the sum of cash required to liquidate the position.

With the stock price below $100, both options expire worthless and so the spread also expires worthless. With the stock price above $100 but below $110, the long call option gives exposure to 100 long units of stock but the short call option gives zero exposure. With the stock price above $110, the higher strike call gives exposure of 100 short units of stock and this completely cancels out the long exposure given by the lower call. So at any stock price above $110, the call spread value is capped at $1,000 and the call spread price will be capped at

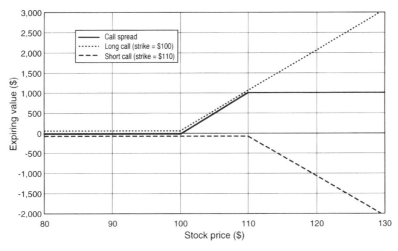

Figure 7.1 Expiring call spread value

$10 per share. The expiring price or value profile below $110 is very much like that of a simple long call position. The addition of the short call position has the effect of removing any further profits above the $110 level, capping the unlimited profit potential of the long option.

It is interesting to consider the spread as one compound investment vehicle. Up until this stage all the financial instruments we have considered have had a price discontinuity or kink at expiry. Treated as

Table 7.1 Expiring call spread value (long one $100 strike call and short one $110 strike call)

Expiring stock price	Long call value (strike = $100) (a)	Short call value (strike = $110) (b)	Call spread value (c) = (a) + (b)	Call spread price (d) = (c)/100
80	0	0	0	0
85	0	0	0	0
90	0	0	0	0
95	0	0	0	0
100	0	0	0	0
105	500	0	+500	+5
110	1,000	0	+1,000	+10
115	1,500	−500	+1,000	+10
120	2,000	−1,000	+1,000	+10
125	2,500	−1,500	+1,000	+10
130	3,000	−2,000	+1,000	+10

Table 7.2   Call spread price one year from expiry

Stock price	Long call price (strike = $100) (a)	Short call price (strike = $110) (b)	Call spread price (c) = (a) + (b)
80	0.40	−0.08	0.32
85	0.98	−0.25	0.73
90	2.02	−0.63	1.39
95	3.67	−1.33	2.34
100	5.98	−2.50	3.48
105	8.95	−4.23	4.72
110	12.50	−6.58	5.92
115	16.52	−9.52	7.00
120	20.89	−13.00	7.89
125	25.50	−16.92	8.58
130	30.28	−21.20	9.08

one entity, the call spread is different in that it has **two kinks** and this makes the price profile before expiry doubly interesting. The price of the call spread prior to expiry can similarly be obtained from the prices of the two separate components. Table 7.2 and Figure 7.2 give the prices of the individual components and the spread for various stock prices one year from expiry.

Call spreads are very popular with outright investors and specula-

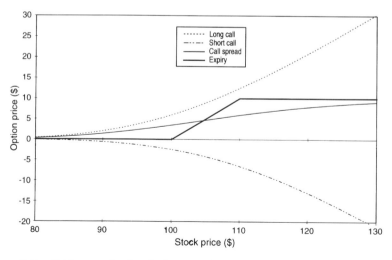

Figure 7.2   Call spread price before expiry

tors because they are cheaper than outright call options and require less of a stock price move to break even. If one believes that the underlying stock price is going to rise significantly in the future one would simply take a long position in the $100 strike call option. However, if one believes that the price rise is not going to be that large, say only 10%, then it may make sense to buy the call spread. The call spread will be cheaper than the outright call option and if the final stock price is not much higher than $110, the final portfolio values will be similar. Since the spread is cheaper, the percentage return will be higher and speculators are usually very concerned about percentage returns. As an example, if the stock price is $100, the outright $100 strike call costs $5.98 but the spread only costs $3.48. If the stock price rises to $110 by expiry, the outright call will be worth $10 producing a profit of 67%, whereas the call spread being worth the same $10 will have produced a profit of 187%. To break even with the outright call option, the underlying stock price must rise to at least $105.98 by expiry, whereas the rise only has to be to $103.48 for the spread. Buying a call spread is less risky than buying an outright call but this is offset by the limited upside potential.

The price of the call spread prior to expiry is curved. At lower stock price levels the price curve sits above the expiry profile and at higher levels the curve sits below the expiry boundary. With one year to expiry the slope of the price curve is very low and in this situation never gets above 0.20. A more detailed study of the various sensitivities of the call spread can be obtained by looking at the price profile at different times to expiry and these are given in Figure 7.3.

The two discontinuities on expiry cause the call spread to have very unusual features, the most interesting one being time decay effects. So far we have discussed portfolios that either suffer from time decay or benefit from time decay. This compound instrument does both. It is clear from Figure 7.3 that below a special stock price ($104 in this case), the passage of time reduces the instrument's value but that above the special price, time passing has the effect of increasing the instrument value. And at one specific price, the instrument is completely independent of time. At first this behaviour seems most peculiar. When you buy a single put or call option, the moment you have bought it, time begins to erode its value. When you sell short a single option, the moment you sell, time begins to act in your favour. With this instrument, the effect depends on the price of the underlying. The reason for this behaviour is of course easy to understand—it is due to

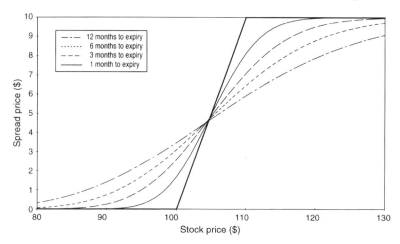

Figure 7.3 Time decay effects on call spread

the fact that the portfolio is simultaneously long and short options with different exercise prices. The net effect of time decay is the sum of the effects of time decay on the individual components. At stock prices lower than $104, the negative time decay effects of the lower call option outweigh the positive time decay effects of the upper call option. At higher prices the reverse is true and at one specific price the two effects match.

As with individual options, the passage of time causes the price curve to move towards the expiry boundary and a study of the way in which the curve moves can shed light on the other option sensitivities. In this case the expiry boundary is more complex and comprises three straight lines with corresponding implications for the sensitivities. The discussion can be reduced to considering the two regions above and below the special stock price of $104.

Lower Region

The price profiles in the lower region are similar to those of a long call option. Along any given curve the deltas are positive and increase with increasing stock price. Time passing has the similar effect of reducing the deltas at lower prices and increasing the deltas at higher prices. The price curvature or gamma is positive and this increases as expiry approaches.

Upper Region

The price profiles in the upper region are similar in shape to those of a short put option. Along any given curve the deltas decrease with increasing stock price. Time passing has the similar effect of increasing the deltas at the lower prices and decreasing the deltas at higher prices. The price curvature is negative and this becomes more pronounced as expiry approaches.

The delta of the combination is always positive or zero and so the appropriate hedge would be a short position in the underlying. Initially the maximum delta is only 0.2 and so the size of the hedge would be quite small. This is due to the fact that a long way from expiry, the two opposing stock exposures almost cancel out. However, the fact that the curvature is positive in the lower region and negative in the upper region, makes things complicated for the volatility player attempting to stay delta neutral. In the lower region, the gamma of the position is positive and so rehedging would entail selling stock on the way up and buying on the way down—the combination is a long volatility position. In the upper region the gamma of the position is negative and so rehedging would entail buying stock on the way up and selling on the way down—the combination is a short volatility position. There is a point on the boundary between the two regions where the curvature or gamma switches from positive to negative, i.e. a point where the gamma is zero and no rehedging would be required. This corresponds to the point with no time decay. At this point the portfolio is neither long nor short volatility and if hedged with the correct amount of short stock, neither long nor short the market.

It may seem strange that someone would want to be in the above position. Until now we have assumed that the individual player, before entering the market, makes a decision about being long or short volatility and so the above combination would not suit. There are situations, however, when the individual may decide that if the market rises, volatility will fall and if the market falls, then volatility will rise. The above combination would perfectly suit such a view. The player would automatically become short volatility on the way up and long volatility on the way down.

Another situation that may make such a combination attractive, is one in which the individual viewed the upper option expensive compared to the lower option. Here the individual has no view on volatility or the direction of the market price but wishes to arbitrage out the difference in option values. In order to do this he must short the expensive option and buy the cheap one. The net combination would be long of the underlying and in order to remove market risk, the appropriate hedge would be used. The portfolio would be run either to expiry or until the apparent anomalous price difference disappeared.

Whatever the reason for entering such a portfolio, it is clear that managing the market hedge and monitoring the effects of time and volatility changes is non-trivial—and this is a relatively simple combination.

7.2   COMBINATION #2: THE TIME SPREAD

This is one of the first strategies introduced to students of options markets. It is simple to understand, appeals to everyone's intuitive notion of time decay and, like the call spread, is low risk. The strategy works with either puts or calls and so for simplicity we will stick to considering calls. The rationale behind the trade comes from diagrams such as Figure 7.4 which illustrate the fact that options suffer most time decay in the final stages of life. Long-dated options do suffer time decay, but at a slower rate than short dated ones. The time spread is an attempt to capitalise on this feature and in its simplest form is a long position in a long-dated option and a short position in a short dated option. The idea is that if the underlying stock price does not move that much, the near option will expire worthless and although the long dated option will have lost some time value, it will not be as much as that lost by the near-dated one.

As an example consider a portfolio long of a 12-month call and short of a 6-month call with both options having the same exercise price of $100. Figure 7.4 shows the price profiles of the individual components and the time spread. In this figure, for ease of exposition, the short option is shown with a positive price. The time spread price is simply the difference between the two curves. We note that initially the portfolio is not particularly interesting. With one option having 12 months to expiry and the other having 6 months, the two will be very similarly priced and so the net position will be very insensitive to changes in stock price and volatility. A better understanding of the rationale behind the trade and the way in which the price sensitivities change can be seen from Figure 7.5 which shows the time spread price

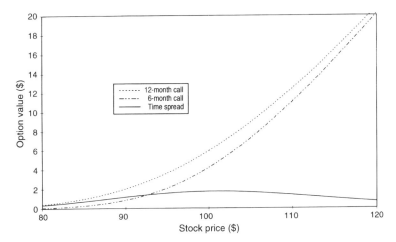

Figure 7.4 Time spread = long 12-month call and short 6-month call

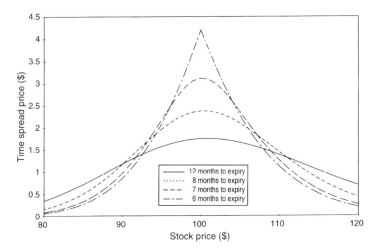

Figure 7.5 Time decay effects on time spread

curves at different times in the future. The curve labelled "6 months elapsed" refers to the day when the long-dated option becomes a 6-month option and the near option expires.

The best possible scenario for the time spread strategy is for the short-dated option to expire exactly at-the-money. In this way the spread which initially has a maximum price of $1.75 ends up priced at $4.20. Between inception of the trade and the expiry of the short-dated option, the time spread price behaviour is very complex. Like the simple call spread, the complexity is due to the portfolio having two expiring price kinks. With the call spread the two kinks are at different prices. With the time spread the kinks are at the same price but at different points in time. Although both curves gradually collapse to the same expiry boundary, they do so at different rates. If the underlying price stays near the exercise price, the price curve is flat and so the portfolio will have no delta and hence no stock exposure. However, either side of the exercise price, the combination begins to get stock exposure. If the stock price rises, the price curve falls and so the overall portfolio becomes short. This could be hedged by buying stock. If the stock price falls lower than the exercise price then the portfolio price also falls and this could be hedged by selling stock. With the stock price near the exercise price, the time spread is in effect short volatility or short gamma. As with most short volatility plays the rehedging losses would be offset by the positive time decay. Deep in-the-money or deep out-of-the-money, the situation reverses. At stock prices far away from the exercise price the time spread has positive gamma and negative time decay. We now consider a more complicated strategy involving three options.

7.3 COMBINATION#3: NEAR-DATED TWO BY ONE RATIO PUT SPREAD WITH FAR-DATED CALL

This is by no means a standard strategy but a combination of two strategies and will be used to illustrate a more complex portfolio. The example portfolio is a short position in two three-month put options with a strike price of $95, a long position in one three-month put option with a strike price of $105 and a long position in one six-month call option with a strike price of $115. The combination has three points of discontinuity, one at $95 and one at $105 in three months' time together with one at $115 in six months' time. The price of the combination is again the sum of the prices of the individual components. This combination is, however, slightly more complex in that the individual position sizes are different. The price of the portfolio is given by

Price of combination = −2 × (price of 3-month put ($95 strike))
+ 1 × (price of 3-month put ($105 strike))
+ 1 × (price of 6-month call ($115 strike))

This will be true of any combination of options involving different position sizes. The price of the combination will be the sum of the individual components weighted by the position sizes. Figure 7.6 shows the price of the example portfolio at various times and stock prices.

At very high and very low stock prices, the combination behaves as if it is simply long of stock and experts in options strategies would know this without the aid of a diagram. The reason is that at very high stock prices, the effects of the puts would be negligible and the call would be so in-the-money as to behave exactly like the underlying stock. At very low prices, the effects of the call would be negligible, the negative stock exposure offered by the $105 long put would be cancelled by one of the short $95 puts and the net position would be simply short the remaining one $95 put, which is of course exactly the same as being long the underlying. Between the two extremes, the price behaviour is complex due to the competing effects of the three different components. Near the stock price of $95, the dominant component would be the short puts. The holder of short options positions benefit from time decay and so the price profile gradually rises. Near the $105 and $115 stock prices the long options have the opposite effect. The six month option will of course decay at a slower rate than the three-month put.

It should be clear from Figure 7.6 where the combination is long or short the market and where the combination is long or short volatility. Below $95 and above $105 the portfolio is essentially long (in various

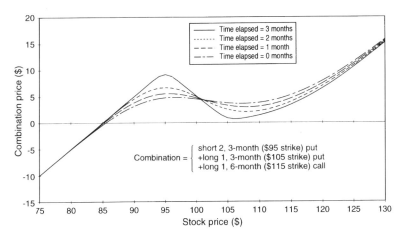

Figure 7.6   Complex combination #3

degrees) the underlying stock and between $95 and $105 the portfolio is short (in various degrees) the underlying stock. The reader should now also be able to recognise a price profile that is long or short volatility. A price profile that has an increasing (decreasing) slope as the underlying price increases is a long (short) volatility curve. This portfolio is long volatility from approximately $100 to $130 and short volatility from $100 to $85.

7.4 THE ADDITIVITY OF SENSITIVITIES

In deriving the price profile of the above combinations, the individual price profiles, weighted for position sizes, were simply added together. This may seem an obvious statement to make but the procedure is valid only because the individual components depend on the price of the underlying stock and not on each other. (The same would not be true of a portfolio containing different stocks.) This concept of **price additivity** can be extended to the most complex portfolios containing large numbers of different positions in put and call options. However, when the number of different positions becomes larger than three, the graphical techniques used above become limited. Eventually one has to resort to some sort of software that can give the price profile of more complicated portfolios. The software given on the disc supplied with this book offers one simple solution. At the core of the software is the Black and Scholes model. We make the assumption that the model prices and price sensitivities accurately reflect what happens in the market-place. For most markets and under most circumstances this assumption is valid.

Recall that the model requires five inputs (ignoring dividend complications): (i) the stock price, (ii) the exercise price, (iii) the time to expiry, (iv) the interest rate and (v) the volatility. For simplicity we restrict consideration to a portfolio containing one given stock and any combination of puts and calls on the stock. Also for simplicity we will use one interest rate and one volatility for all the options under consideration. (We address the more complex aspects of using different interest rates and volatility for different options later.) The process involves substituting the different exercise prices and expiry times into the model and adding (or subtracting if short) the various output prices in the appropriate sizes. Thus a portfolio long one option priced at $3.50, short two options priced at $1.25 and long three options priced at $1.00 would be priced at

Combination price = 1 × 3.50 − 2 × 1.25 + 3 × 1.00 = 4.00 (7.1)

For any general portfolio the price would be given by

Combination price = (size #1) × (price #1)
+ (size #2) × (price #2) + ... etc. (7.2)

This general additivity of position prices lends itself particularly to simple spreadsheet type software. All one needs is the ability to calculate the model prices and even these can be simply calculated on a spreadsheet. It is thus possible to recalculate the combination price for any number of different stock prices and times to expiry and plot the results. The flexibility of spreadsheets means that the novice can experiment with different volatilities and interest rates to see the effects these have on the most complicated portfolios. Most of the figures shown in this book were obtained using the given software.

Deriving the price profile of a combination is very useful and with experience, most volatility players will have a fairly good idea even without the use of software. What is probably more important is to be able to derive the various sensitivity profiles accurately. An option fund manager will want to know exactly how long or short of the market he is. If he is long volatility he will want to know when he needs to rehedge or what the gamma of his portfolio is. If he is short volatility he will need to know the time decay he will earn every day (his theta) and what the likely rehedging losses are. Also he will need to know how all these factors will alter if the underlying stock price is different tomorrow or next week or if the market suddenly becomes more volatile. In short, the manager will not only need to know the portfolio price, but also all the portfolio sensitivities to changes in stock price, time and volatility.

The problem is a lot easier than it first looks and this is again because of the simplicity offered by the additivity of prices. Individual option sensitivities are rates of changes of prices and since the price of a combination is the sum of the individual option prices, the sensitivity of a combination of options will be the sum of the individual sensitivities. So in the example given by expression (7.1), if the option deltas are 0.40, 0.30 and 0.1 respectively, the delta of the combination is given by

Combination delta = 1 $\times$ 0.40 $-$ 2 $\times$ 0.30 + 3 $\times$ 0.1 = +0.1   (7.3)

The portfolio has a delta of 0.1 and so would behave identically to one long of $0.1 \times 100 = 10$ units of stock. For any general portfolio the delta would be given by

Combination delta = (size#1) $\times$ (delta#1)
+ (size#2) $\times$ (delta#2) + ... etc.   (7.2)

This concept can be applied to all of the sensitivities such as gamma, theta and vega and means that the calculation of the total portfolio risk involves nothing more mathematically complex than **summation**.

7.5   MONITORING THE RISK OF A COMPLEX OPTIONS PORTFOLIO

Looking at price profiles such as Figures 7.1–7.6 is useful for getting an overall feel for how the value of a portfolio changes with stock price and time. However, it is usually necessary to have much more detailed breakdown of all the risks a portfolio is exposed to and these risks need to be expressed in dollar terms. To illustrate one way in which the risks can be examined we return to combination #3 example given above. In order to make the numbers more meaningful we multiply all the position sizes by 100. The example portfolio thus comprises a short position in 200 three-month $95 strike puts, long 100 three-month $105 strike puts and long 100 six-month $115 strike calls. For simplicity we assume that all options were purchased or sold at the appropriate fair value using a volatility of 15% when the stock price was $100 and that interest rates are zero. Initially it is necessary to define three shift parameters: a volatility shift, a time shift and a stock price shift. These parameters will set the risk definitions associated with changes in the relevant variable.

Volatility Shift

A major source of risk to an options portfolio is the change in the overall market price of volatility. In the example portfolio we are assuming that the portfolio is set up when all options are trading at prices derived by using an input volatility of 15%. What if this suddenly increases by a given amount, say 1% to 16%? The given amount is the volatility shift used to define such volatility (or vega) risk and throughout the rest of this book we will set this to 1% although it is possible to use any figure. Columns headed (+ vol) will refer to the changes caused by increasing the volatility by 1%.

Time Shift

The time shift parameter in the illustrated example is set to 1 day (1/365th of a year) but of course can be set to a longer time period. This means that when reading the risk table, the columns headed (+ time) will refer to the changes caused by the passage of one day.

Stock Price Shift

Whether long or short volatility, the portfolio manager will need to have an idea as to how rapidly the delta of the portfolio is changing with respect to changes in the underlying stock price, i.e. the position gamma. Rather than give an instantaneous rate of change it is useful to have a measure that gives the difference in position delta when the underlying moves a specific amount—the stock price shift. In this example we set the stock price shift to the very small value of $0.10.

The two main concerns are (i) how does the value of the portfolio change and (ii) how does the stock exposure of the portfolio change? Table 7.3 gives the risk breakdown of the example portfolio and is divided into two sections. The left-hand side gives the profit and loss in dollars and the right-hand side gives information about the total market exposure in stock units. We first discuss the elements of the row corresponding to the stock price of $100.

- **Profit and Loss = 0**. The total portfolio value at $100 is $45,572. The portfolio was constructed with the stock price at $100, so the prices will not have changed and therefore the net profit at this level is zero.

- **Profit and Loss (+ vol) = −$144**. This figure of −$144 represents the change in the overall profit if volatility were to increase by the amount defined by the volatility shift parameter. So, other things being equal, if all the volatilities increase by 1%, the portfolio will drop in value by $144. Similarly, other things being equal, if all the volatilities decrease by 1%, the portfolio would increase in value by $144.

Table 7.3 Risk statistics: - 200 × (3-month $95 puts) + 100 × (3-month $105 puts) + 100 × (6-month $115 calls). Vol shift = 1%, time shift = 1 day, stock price shift = $0.10, portfolio value at $100 = $45,572

	Profit and loss ($)			Equivalent stock position (stock units)			
Stock price	Profit	Profit (+ vol)	Profit (+ time)	ESP	ESP (+ vol)	ESP (+ time)	Gamma
76	−135,620	−36	+3	+9,970	−20	+2	−2
80	−96,027	−231	+20	+9,977	−90	+8	−10
84	−58,231	−848	+72	+8,970	−222	+19	−33
88	−25,923	−1,904	+164	+6,945	−273	+24	−69
92	−4,396	−2,656	+235	+3,673	−54	+7	−90
96	+3,302	−2,089	+203	+300	+341	−23	−72
100	**0**	**−144**	**+65**	**−1,611**	**+582**	**−42**	**−21**
104	−6,707	+2,132	−95	−1,409	+508	−35	+29
108	−9,186	+3,682	−196	+343	+256	−15	+55
112	−3,260	+4,215	−221	+2,636	+25	+1	+57
116	**+11,649**	**+4,017**	**−198**	**+4,755**	**−107**	**+9**	**+48**
120	+34,182	+3,463	−160	+6,432	−160	+10	+36
124	+62,511	+2,788	−122	+7,664	−172	+9	+26

- **Profit and Loss (+ time)** = **+$65**. This is the change in the portfolio value caused by one day passing. So, other things being equal, the portfolio will increase in value by $65 by the next day.

These sums are small compared to the overall portfolio value, because at this stock price the positive and negative effects of the volatility changes and time decay on the prices of the individual components almost completely cancel out. A breakdown of the effects of these changes on the individual components is shown in Table 7.4.

- **ESP** = **−1,611 stock units**. The equivalent stock position (ESP) gives the net exposure of the position. At $100 this is −1,611 and so the position would feel as if the portfolio were short of 1,611 units of stock. A volatility player not interested in being exposed to the direction of the underlying could of course remove this risk by buying 1,611 units of stock.

- **ESP(+ vol)** = **+582 stock units**. This represents the change in the stock exposure caused by a general increase in volatility. Other things being equal, if the volatility increases by 1%, the exposure increases by 582 units and so the resultant exposure would now be = −1,611 + 582 = −1,029 units. If the volatility decreased by 1% the exposure would decrease by 582 units resulting in an exposure of −1,611 − 582 = −2,193 units.

- **ESP(+ time)** = **−42 stock units**. This represents the change in the exposure with the passage of time. At this stock price level, the exposure of this portfolio will decrease by 42 stock units to $-1,611 - 42 = -1653$ units the next day.

- **Gamma** = **−21 stock units**. This represents the level of rehedging activity necessary to stay delta neutral or the rate at which the stock exposure is altering. At a stock price near $100 this portfolio would require adjustments of 21 units per $0.10 move The negative sign indicates that at this level the portfolio is short volatility and so small increases (decreases) in stock price would require buying (selling) 21 units per $0.10 move.

In summary then, at $100 the portfolio will suffer a small loss if volatility increases and gain in value with the passage of time. At $100 the position is slightly short of the market and slightly short of volatility. We now consider the effects on the same portfolio of the (slightly unrealistic) situation of the stock price suddenly increasing to $116.

- **Profit and Loss** = **+11,649**. The portfolio will have increased in value by $11,649.

- **Profit and Loss (+ vol)** = **+$4,017**. This is saying that if the volatility increases by 1% there will be an additional profit of $4,017 and so the total profit would now be that due to the price move plus that due to the volatility move or 11,649 + 4,017 = $15,666. If, however, the volatility falls by 1% the profit would be reduced by 4,017 = to $7,632. If the volatility were to alter by more than 1%, the effect on the overall profit would be significant. At this stock level the vega risk to the portfolio is much larger than at $100.

- **Profit and Loss (+ time)** = **−$198**. The time decay at this stock price level is now −$198 per day. These losses would be subtracted from the corresponding profit of $11,649.

- **ESP** = **+4,755 stock units**. At this level the portfolio has an exposure of long 4,755 stock units and this will increase with increasing stock price. In the limit, at very high stock prices, this figure will approach a maximum of 10,000 and is all due to the long 100 call options.

- **ESP(+ vol)** = **−107 stock units**. Other things being equal, the exposure will decrease by 107 units if the volatility increases by 1%. So at a volatility of 16% the net stock exposure would be = 4,755 − 107 = 4,648 units.

- **ESP(+ time)** = **+9 stock units**. Time passing will increase the stock exposure by 9 units a day.

- **Gamma** = **+48 stock units**. Up at this level, the gamma is positive and equal to 48 stock units per $0.10 price move. The move from $100 to $116 has resulted in the portfolio changing from one of short volatility to one of long volatility. At $100 the negative curvature of the 200 short puts dominates the portfolio, whereas at $116 the dual effects of the positive curvature of the long $105 put and the long $115 call dominate.

Software that produces risk tables like that given in Table 7.3 allow an options manager to predict, with a fair degree of confidence, what will happen to his portfolio at any stock price and if market conditions change. More importantly, the output allows a volatility player to see, before it happens, how his hedging activity will alter under a variety of different scenarios. In addition to giving the overall portfolio characteristics, it is sometimes instructive to look in more detail at the contribution of each of the individual components to the total. Since the total portfolio characteristics are simply the sum of the individual characteristics the examination of such breakdowns is straightforward. The software produces subsets of individual characteristics like those in Table 7.4 showing the contributions to the total vega and theta effects on the profit.

Table 7.4 Breakdown of profit changes at stock price = $100

Option	Position (a)	Vega risk (volatility increase by 1%)		Theta risk (time decrease by one day)	
		One option (b)	Portfolio size (c) = (a) × (b)	One option (d)	Portfolio size (e) = (a) × (d)
3-month ($95) put	−200	+15.22	−3,044	−1.27	+254
3-month ($105) put	+100	+16.37	+1,637	−1.37	−137
6-month ($115) call	+100	+12.63	+1,263	−0.52	−52
Total			**−$144**		**+$65**

7.6 ADJUSTING THE RISK PROFILE OF AN OPTION PORTFOLIO

Say the portfolio manager lets the above position run unhedged to the point at which the underlying stock price is $116. At this level he will have a mark to market (i.e. unrealised) profit of $11,649 and have a portfolio that has long stock exposure of 4,755 units. Say at this level the manager no longer wishes to be long of the market and wishes to apply a hedge. What should he do? The simplest solution would be to short 4,755 stock units and Table 7.5 gives the risk characteristics of the hedged portfolio. Comparing Table 7.5 with the unhedged portfolio given in Table 7.3, we see that the only difference is in the ESP and profit columns; all other risk characteristics are the same. Shorting 4,755 stock units has the effect of reducing the exposure by 4,755 units at all price levels and since stock has no price curvature or gamma, the sensitivities to volatility and/or time are unaffected. The only changes to the profit side are those associated with an addition of stock short at $116. If the underlying price falls all the way down to $100 again, the net profit would increase by 4,755 × (116 − 100) = $76,080. The change in the risk caused by shorting stock can be best illustrated graphically by considering Figure 7.7. This chart shows the price profile of the hedged and unhedged portfolio at the time of inception. At $116, the unhedged portfolio has a slope of 4,755 units and the hedged portfolio has a slope of zero. Hedging with straightforward stock has the effect of rotating the entire price profile until the slope at $116 is reduced to zero. It also has the effect of reducing the slope (i.e. exposure) of the curve everywhere by 4,755 units.

Table 7.5   Combination #3 hedged with short stock
−200 × (3-month $95 puts) + 100 × (3-month $105 puts) + 100 × (6-month $115 calls) −4,755 units of stock

| Stock price | Profit and loss ($) | | | Equivalent stock position (stock units) | | | |
	Profit	Profit (+ vol)	Profit (+ time)	ESP	ESP (+ vol)	ESP (+ time)	Gamma
76	+54,580	−36	+3	+5,215	−20	+2	−2
80	+75,153	−231	+20	+5,018	−90	+8	−10
84	+93,929	−848	+72	+4,215	−222	+19	−33
88	+107,217	−1,904	+164	+2,190	−273	+24	−69
92	+109,724	−2,656	+235	−1,082	−54	+7	−90
96	+98,402	−2,089	+203	−4,455	+341	−23	−72
100	**+76,080**	**−144**	**+65**	**−6,366**	**+582**	**−42**	**−21**
104	+50,353	+2,132	−95	−6,164	+508	−35	+29
108	+28,854	+3,682	−196	−4,412	+256	−15	+55
112	+15,760	+4,215	−221	−2,119	+25	+1	+57
116	**+11,649**	**+4,017**	**−198**	**0**	**−107**	**+9**	**+48**
120	+15,162	+3,463	−160	+1,677	−160	+10	+36
124	+24,471	+2,788	−122	+2,909	−172	+9	+26

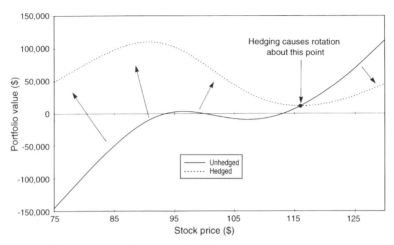

Figure 7.7   Hedging combination #3 with short stock

Using short stock has had the desired effect of removing the market risk around the $116 level but all of the other risk characteristics are unaffected. At $116 the portfolio is still long of volatility and will lose $198 a day. The manager may be happy with this situation but he may want to remove some of the time decay risk and vega risk as well as removing the market risk. To do this he has to consider hedging not with stock but with other options. One possibility is to short a call option and for simplicity we restrict attention to the near dated calls with strike prices in the range $105–$125. Table 7.6 lists the characteristics of these instruments assuming a position size of 100.

A short position in any of these call options in the right size will remove the market risk in the immediate vicinity of $116 and all will reduce, to some extent, the vega and theta risk. Which one the man-

Table 7.6   Risk characteristics of 3-month call per 100 options at stock price = $116

Exercise price	Option value ($)	Stock exposure stock units	Vega per 1% Change ($)	Theta Per Day ($)
105	113,500	9,154	893	74
110	71,800	7,735	1,734	145
115	39,500	5,610	2,271	189
120	18,600	3,380	2,106	175
125	7,400	1,670	1,441	120

ager will choose will depend on his risk preferences. As an example consider using the $110 strike call option. Shorting 100 of these options will provide a market short equivalent to 7,735 stock units. We only need a short of 4,755 units and so the appropriate number of options would be given by:

$$\text{Number of short \$110 call options to give 4,755 negative stock exposure} = 100 \times \frac{4,755}{7,735}$$
$$= 61$$

Accordingly, we sell short 61 of these options, taking in 61 × (71,800)/100 = $43,798 of premium. It is also possible to calculate, before we implement this hedge, the reduction in vega and theta risk. If 100 of these options have a vega of $1,734 and a theta of $145, then by a similar calculation, 61 options will have vegas and thetas of $1,058 and $88 respectively. So shorting 61 of the three-month $110 strike call options will have the dual effects of removing the market risk in the vicinity of $116 and reducing the time decay and vega risk. The total risk profile for this portfolio is given in Table 7.7 and a graphical illustration of the effect of using the short calls is given in Figure 7.8.

Table 7.7 Combination #3 hedged with short call options
(−200 × (3-month $95 puts) + 100 × (3-month $105 puts) + 100 × (6-month $115 calls) − 61 × (3-month $110 calls))

	Profit and loss ($)			Equivalent stock position (stock units)			
Stock price	Profit	Profit (+ vol)	Profit (+ time)	ESP	ESP (+ vol)	ESP (+ time)	Gamma
76	−91,850	−36	+3	+9,970	−20	+2	−2
80	−52,257	−231	+20	+9,773	−90	+8	−10
84	−14,463	−850	+72	+8,969	−223	+19	−33
88	+17,830	−1,918	+165	+6,935	−279	+25	−69
92	+39,249	−2,724	+240	+3,617	−78	+9	−92
96	+46,451	−2,323	+223	+76	+280	−18	−78
100	**+41,505**	**−703**	**+112**	**−2,264**	**+483**	**−33**	**−36**
104	+30,724	+1,159	−14	−2,855	+409	−27	+4
108	+20,335	+2,405	−90	−2,202	+211	−11	+25
112	+13,709	+2,913	−112	−1,084	+57	−1	+29
116	**+11,649**	**+2,959**	**−110**	**37**	**−24**	**+2**	**+27**
120	+13,829	+2,762	−102	+1,028	−72	+2	+23
124	+19,673	+2,401	−90	+1,868	−107	+3	+19

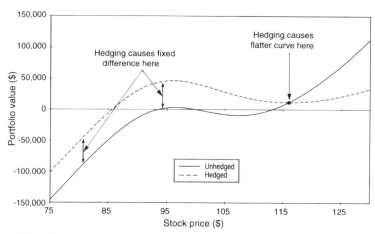

Figure 7.8 Hedging combination #3 with short calls

We see that hedging using the short call options has the desired effect in the region near $116. At $116 the price curve now has the desired slope of (near) zero and the curvature is less marked. The gamma of the position has fallen from +48 to +27. Note that at lower stock prices these effects wear off and this is due to the nature of a short call option profile. The most one can make selling call options is the premium taken in. At very low stock prices the only difference between the hedged and the unhedged position is the $43,798 call premium. This is only one example of using short calls to hedge and it is left as an exercise for the reader to see what the effect would be using other strike prices.

A third solution to the original hedging problem of removing the long stock exposure is to buy put options. Consider the six-month put

Table 7.8 Risk characteristics of 6-month put per 100 options at stock price = $116

Exercise price	Option value ($)	Stock exposure stock units	Vega per 1% change ($)	Theta per day ($)
105	10,882	−1,602	1,995	82
110	23,597	−2,897	2,803	115
115	43,946	−4,464	3,238	133
120	72,368	−6,053	3,153	130
125	108,041	−7,430	2,641	109

characteristics given in Table 7.8: 100 of the $125 strike puts give negative stock exposure of 7,430 units. We only need 4,755 short stock units to neutralise combination 3 and so the required number is given by:

$$\text{Number of \$125 put options to give 4,755 negative stock exposure} = 100 \times \frac{4,755}{7,430}$$

$$= 64$$

Using similar calculations it is possible to show that 64 long put options will increase the vega and theta by $1,690 and $70 respectively.

Table 7.9 and Figure 7.9 give the risk characteristics of the hedged portfolio. As predicted, the vega and theta have increased as has the gamma. At $116 the portfolio is now long 65 gamma and this is clear from the increased curvature. Using long puts has the complete reverse effect of using short calls. At very low stock prices, the long 64 puts will kick in 100% and give 64 × 100 = 6,400 negative stock exposure units. If the stock price rises, the long $115 call options are free to increase in value and will have no short call or short stock to limit the upside. Using put options to hedge will increase the profits if the stock rises or falls. The downside is that the theta decay is much larger. Hedging with long puts has simply increased the degree of long

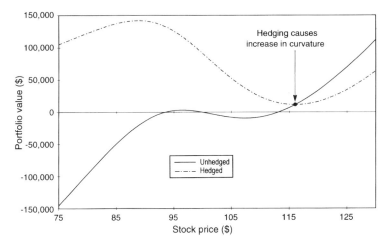

Figure 7.9 Hedging combination #3 with long puts

volatility. Figure 7.10 illustrates the three different hedging strategies. The manager will choose which to use on the basis of his view on market volatility.

Table 7.9 Combination #3 hedged with long put options $-200 \times$ (3-month $95 puts) + $100 \times$ (3-month $105 puts) + $100 \times$ (6-month $115 calls) + $64 \times$ (6-month $125 puts)

	Profit and loss ($)			Equivalent stock position (stock units)			
Stock price	Profit	Profit (+ vol)	Profit (+ time)	ESP	ESP (+ vol)	ESP (+ time)	Gamma
76	+108,834	−36	+3	+3,570	−20	+2	−2
80	+122,827	−231	+20	+3,373	−90	+8	−10
84	+135,024	−847	+72	+2,571	−222	+19	−33
88	+141,740	−1,897	+163	+548	−270	+24	−68
92	+137,698	−2,627	+233	−2,713	−45	+7	−89
96	+119,908	−2,001	+200	−6,053	+363	−24	−70
100	**+91,334**	**+74**	**+56**	**−7,883**	**+627**	**−43**	**−18**
104	+59,838	+2,586	−114	−7,513	+582	−38	+34
108	+33,482	+4,489	−229	−5,467	+357	−19	+64
112	+17,016	+5,459	−272	−2,723	+139	−3	+70
116	**+11,649**	**+5,708**	**−268**	**0**	**−3**	**+4**	**+65**
120	+16,576	+5,510	−245	+2,399	−90	+7	+55
124	+30,316	+5,023	−215	+4,405	−150	+8	+45

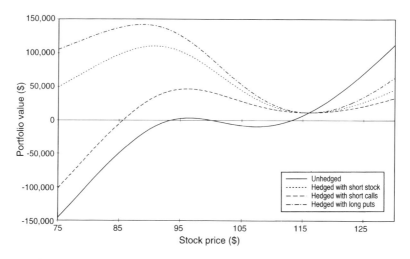

Figure 7.10 Alternative hedging strategies for combination #3

7.7 APPROXIMATE DIRECTION RISK ASSESSMENT

Software like that supplied with this book is very useful at accurately estimating the various types of risk associated with complex portfolios. However, there are approximate techniques that give a rough estimate of the position risk that does not require the use of software. Managers running several different option portfolios find these methods useful for getting a quick overview of the extreme risks associated with large stock price moves. If a portfolio has a large number of different longs and shorts in puts and calls, one quick method is to ignore time decay and volatility effects and assume that all options will trade at intrinsic value. This is really only valid near expiration and/or with very low volatility but the method does give a good idea of the directional risks associated with large price moves. With large price moves one can be sure that all options will be either deep in-the-money or deep out-of-the money. In almost all circumstances, deep-in-the-money options trade at intrinsic value and hence give the maximum stock exposure possible and deep out-of-the-money options are worthless and so have zero stock exposure.

Starting with call options the procedure is as follows. If all options trade at intrinsic value, then long call positions will have a stock exposure of +100 units above the strike price and zero below. Short call positions will have a stock exposure of −100 above the strike price and zero below. As an example, consider the portfolio of call options given in Figure 7.11 in which we use the usual notation of a + indicating a long position and a − indicating a short position. Note the two extreme stock exposures of each option either side of each strike price. Begin with the option with the lowest strike price. Below the lowest strike, consider all calls to have zero exposure. Above the first strike price the exposure will be equal to the exposure of the lowest call (in this case long 300 units). Go to the next strike up and add the exposure of this position to the existing position. So at the $95 strike the exposure below $95 is long 300 units, but above, it is short 100 units. Go to the next strike and continue until the last option. We see that at any price above $110 the portfolio is short 300 units. The figures between each strike price give a rough estimate of the likely exposure if the options trade at intrinsic value. The figures can also be used to give a rough estimate of the likely profit or loss to a portfolio. If the manager is considering the portfolio at a time when the stock

Portfolio of five different call options

Strike price	$90	$95	$100	$105	$110
Call position	+3	-4	+3	-1	-4

----------| $90| ----------| $95| --------| $100| --------|$105| ---------| $110|-----------

Position sizes: +3   -4   +3   -1   -4   × (+100)

Stock exposures: 0 | +300   0 | -400   0 | +300   0 | -100   0 | -400
of components

Total exposures: 0 | +300 | -100 | +200 | +100 | -300
of call portfolio

Portfolio of five different put options

Strike price	$90	$95	$100	$105	$110
Put position	-6	+8	-2	-3	+3

----------| $90| ----------| $95| ---------| $100| --------|$105| ---------| $110|-----------

Position sizes: -6   +8   -2   -3   +3   × (-100)

Stock exposures: +600 | 0   -800 | 0   +200 | 0   +300 | 0   -300 | 0
of components

Total exposures: 0 | -600 | +200 | 0 | -300 | 0
of put portfolio

Total exposures   0 | **-300** | **+100** | **+200** | **-200** | **-300**
of portfolio

Figure 7.11   Combination #4

price is $100 then a move to $105 at an exposure of +200 units would represent a gain of 200 ×5 = +$1,000. A drop in price to $95 would represent a gain (because exposure is negative below $95) of 100 × 5 = $500. Profits or losses associated with larger stock price moves can be obtained by simply adding the relevant exposures times the strike price interval.

With put options the procedure is the reverse. We use the put portfolio in Figure 7.11 as an illustration. Each long put option gives exposure to −100 units below the exercise price and zero above. Each short put option gives exposure to +100 units below the exercise price and zero above. Multiplying each position size by the relevant exposure gives the individual contributions. To find the total exposure start at the highest strike price. Above the highest strike price ($110) all puts will have zero exposure. Below the highest strike, the exposure will be equal to that of the put option (−300 units in this case). Go to the second highest strike price ($105). This position is short 3 puts and so contributes +300 stock units below $105. Add the stock exposure of this put to the existing position and the result is 0 or no exposure. Repeat the procedure until below the lowest strike. Finally, add the exposures of the puts and calls together along with any stock and the result gives overall directional risk of the combination. This particular example, which we shall refer to as combination #4, is short the market above $105 and between $90 and $95 and long between $95 and $105 and neutral below $90.

It should be noted that this approach to risk management is only approximate. If the time to expiry is more than a few weeks and the implied volatilities of the options are not small, then one cannot assume that all the options will trade at intrinsic value. However, the technique gives very good directional risk estimates for large price moves. The above portfolio is exposed to the risk of a large stock price change.

7.8   APPROXIMATE VOLATILITY RISK ASSESSMENT

In certain circumstances it is possible to get an approximate idea if a portfolio is long or short volatility without the use of sophisticated software. As explained in section 6.5, the volatility player views puts and calls identically; he is only concerned with the degree of positive or negative price curvature. All one needs to know is if the portfolio is long or short options. The netting off procedure offers a very convenient method and to illustrate, we return to combination #4. The portfolio is reproduced along with the net options positions in Table 7.10.

For the volatility trade we are most interested in the gamma of the combination at various stock prices. In any options portfolio the gamma of the total is the sum of the gamma of the individual parts. Each negative effect will be offset by a corresponding positive effect. Each short option position will contribute a negative gamma and each

Table 7.10 Net option position of combination #4

Strike price	$90	$95	$100	$105	$110	Total
Call position	+3	−4	+3	−1	−4	
Put position	−6	+8	−2	−3	+3	
Net position	**−3**	**+4**	**+1**	**−4**	**−1**	**−3**

long option position will contribute a positive gamma. The net gamma at any particular stock price will depend on the relative magnitude of the gammas of the individual components. Recall from Figure 4.11 that the gamma of an option is maximum (or minimum if short) if the option is near-the-money. Also the absolute size of the maximum (minimum) gamma depends on the time to expiration. If the option only has a short time to live, say one month or less, the change in gamma near-the-money is large. If the option has some time to expire, say three months or more, the gamma profile is relatively flat. This has implications for the way in which one can informally look at net option positions. If the options are near expiry, the gamma effects will be concentrated around each strike price whereas if the expiry date is some time in the future, the gamma effects will be much more diffuse and not concentrated at particular strike prices. The significant option positions of combination #4 are short the $90 and $105 strike and long the $95 strike. With only one month or so to expiry, combination #4 will be short volatility near the $90 and $105 strike and long volatility near the $95 strike. With three months to expiry, the gamma effects of the individual options are so small and similar that one can simply assume that they are all the same and thus consider the portfolio as containing just the total net options position, i.e. = −3. Three months or more from expiry the overall portfolio is simply short three options and will have a small degree of negative curvature. These comments are illustrated by the price profiles shown in Figure 7.12.

7.9 VOLATILITY TRADES AND MARKET MANIPULATION

Volatility traders are from time to time accused of causing abnormal stock price movements or market manipulation. To see why it would make sense to manipulate a market, consider the situation of two

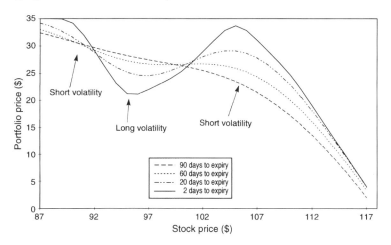

Figure 7.12 Complex combination #4

traders; one long volatility and the other short volatility. To make the illustration simple let us assume that the respective portfolios contain only one option—the $100 stock call option, hedged with stock. Let us first consider the situation of the long volatility player. He is long the call option and short the underlying. He hopes that from inception to expiry the underlying stock price fluctuates wildly. If the fluctuations occur around the exercise price, his profits will be even greater. With the stock price near the exercise price, the gamma will be maximum, necessitating a large number of rehedging trades, each one locking in a profit. Now consider the situation very near the expiry date, say with only one week or only one day to go. Options suffer the most time decay in the final stages of life and particularly if the stock price is near the exercise price. There is always the danger that if the option is still at-the-money by this final stage, that the volatility will suddenly die. The worst case scenario for the long volatility player is for the option to expire at-the-money (see Figure 4.16). The individual has a vested interest in the option expiring either in-the-money or out-of-the-money, particularly if the final price move is sudden.

To see the profits that can be made in the final stages of an options life consider the situation, if with one day before expiry, the stock price is $99.9 and the portfolio is long 100 options. At this price and assuming a volatility of 15%, the option will be priced at $0.27 and have a delta of 0.45. The option will be hedged with $0.45 \times 100 \times 100 = 4,500$ short stock units. The option portion will be worth $0.27 \times 100 \times 100 = \$2,700$

and this will be the sum lost if the stock price is at or below $100 on expiry. If the stock price suddenly moved either up or down before expiry and the hedge was left unaltered, a significant profit would result. Table 7.11 shows the profits with two different price moves.

So the holder of this portfolio would be very pleased if the stock price suddenly moved away from the exercise price just before expiry. Rather than hope for natural causes, some players have been known to help the stock price move by either putting in large buy or sell orders just prior to expiry. In some cases the market may not need much of a nudge when one remembers that for every long option position there is also a short option position and if the other side of this trade is a short volatility portfolio then pushing the stock price one way may have a chain reaction effect. To keep delta neutral, the individual short of volatility must sell stock if the price falls. In the above example if the stock price is pushed from $99.9 to $99.5 this may be enough to trigger a sell signal from the short volatility player. Further selling may trigger more selling with the result that the price may fall significantly by expiry. And this may all have been started by the long volatility player putting in a relatively small sell order.

The interesting point about the issue of market manipulation is that the long volatility player, by definition, should buy if the underlying price falls and sell if it rises. To manipulate a stock price down he must sell into a falling market and to manipulate a stock price up he must buy into a rising market—exactly the opposite strategy the trade dictates. So if a long volatility player decides to manipulate the market he must be sure that the costs of manipulation do not exceed the projected profits.

Now consider the other individual—the short volatility player. His best possible scenario is for the option to expire exactly at-the-money

Table 7.11 Expiring profit to long volatility trade (portfolio = long 100 options at $0.27 and short 4,500 stock at $99.9)

	Stock price down to $98	Stock price up to $102
Option profit	$100 \times 100 \times (0 - 0.27) =$ $-\$2,700$	$100 \times 100 \times (+ 2 - 0.27) =$ $+\$17,300$
Stock profit	$4,500 \times (99.9 - 98.0) =$ $+ \$8,550$	$4,500 \times (99.9 - 102.0) =$ $-\$9,450$
Total profit	$+\$5,850$	$+\$7,850$

(see Figure 5.6). In the final stages of the option's life it is in his best interests to manipulate the stock price so that it stays as near the exercise price as possible. If the stock price begins to fall away from the strike price then he would need to buy in order to try to support the market and possibly bring the stock price back up to the exercise price. If the stock price begins to rise significantly above the strike price, it would be in his interest to sell stock in order to stop the rise and possibly force the price back down again. But in order to stay delta neutral, a short volatility player should be selling on the way down and buying on the way up. If he decides to manipulate the market, the short volatility player, like the long volatility player, is breaking the rules that will keep him delta neutral and such action will result in an exposure to directional risk. Manipulating the market can result in losing large sums of money.

There is definite evidence that in some markets, options expiry coincides with unusual price moves. In the US index options markets, certain expiry days, when more than one type of option expire, are referred to as triple witching days. In the early 1990s large players involved in the Nikkei 225 Index Options Market in Osaka were responsible for moves of up to 5% overnight. Often two opposing investment houses would take huge positions in options with just 12 hours of life left and place huge buy or sell orders in the underlying equity markets. On expiry one house would make $20 million at the expense of another and at the next expiry the same house would lose $20 million. To the smaller individuals in the market, it was like watching the clash of the Titans.

Probably the most famous example of market manipulation is the one that caused the downfall of England's oldest merchant bank— Barings. By February 1995 the Barings trader in the Nikkei 225 Index Futures and Options pit in Singapore (the SIMEX market) had acquired enormous short positions in index options. These options were exercisable into index futures contracts. (We do not intend to go into the details of futures contracts here but just note a long futures contract has exactly the same risk as a long position in the underlying basket of stocks. If one is long a futures contract and the market falls then losses will result.) The trader had a huge short volatility position—possibly the largest short volatility position in equity options ever held by anyone. The previous year had been one of the most stable in recent times. The Nikkei 225 Index had traded in a very narrow range of + or −5% for over six months and the trader was betting that this would continue. Unfortunately on 25 February an earthquake struck mainland Japan.

Equity fund managers were puzzled when the Nikkei 225 Index Futures Market did not immediately fall. The earthquake was believed to have serious implications for equity market valuation and most participants expected a fall of at least 5%. Many had begun to sell futures heavily in the expectation of a market crash and were bemused at the ease of execution—there seemed to be a mysterious buyer, and a buyer in very large size. The Barings trader was very short volatility and if the market had fallen, would have had to have sold enormous numbers of futures contracts to stay neutral. He realised that his rehedging activity would have to be so large that it would have precipitated an even larger market crash than was expected as a result of the earthquake and so he decided to try to manipulate the entire Japanese equity market—he bought futures rather than sold. And this was why the market did not immediately fall. The Barings trader was buying in the face of the large selling pressure from all over the world. It worked for a few days. Over the course of the next week the Barings trader accumulated tens of thousands of long futures contracts in an attempt to prop up the market. Eventually the trader ran out of money and in his own words, could no longer support the market. When the problem became public knowledge, the rest of the market knew that the Bank of England (on behalf of Barings who were in liquidation) would be a panic seller and the market promptly dropped 1,000 points. To date the losses are estimated to be £860 million and the fiasco sent one of the world's most respected banks under. And all because of a short volatility trade that got out of hand. It may be possible to manipulate a given stock but to try to hold up the world's second largest equity market against natural forces was very ambitious.

There is a final point worth making in the wake of the Barings collapse and that is the question of the losses. The media at the time were obsessed with the size of the losses and they certainly were very large. But no one seems to have mentioned the profits. The futures and options business is a zero sum game. For every dollar lost there is a dollar made. If Barings lost £860 million then someone made £860 million and no one seems to have bothered to mention this. Barings were short volatility to the rest of the world being long volatility and these individuals quietly banked their profits. No money was lost. All that happened was that £860 million changed hands.

7.10   SYNTHETIC OPTIONS FROM DYNAMIC TRADING OF STOCK

In section 6.5 we demonstrated how it is possible to synthesise a long put option position from a long call option position and short stock. We also showed how it was possible to synthesise a call from a put and stock and that in fact all one needs is any two instruments and one can generate the third. Synthesising one instrument from the other two is essentially transforming the one expiring discontinuity into a different form. But what if there are no listed puts or calls on the stock of interest? If we have no instrument with a price discontinuity where do we start? Here we show that it is not even necessary to have an exchange traded options market—one can synthesise an option position by simply dynamically trading the stock.

To illustrate how this is done we consider three fund managers A, B and C. Managers A and B jointly run a delta neutral short volatility portfolio and manager C runs a speculative fund. All three individuals are interested in the stock in question that is currently trading at $99 and has a one-year call option with an exercise price of $100 that is trading at an implied volatility of 15%, i.e. a price of $5.46. The delta of the option is 0.50 and so the hedged portfolio initially consists of short one call option and long 50 units of stock—this is the initial set-up described in Chapter 5.

A and B are responsible for the two different elements of the short volatility portfolio. A monitors the price of the short call option and does nothing else. B is responsible for the rehedging activity, buying with a price rise and selling with a price fall. Let us assume that A and B keep separate records of profits. C believes the stock price is going to rise by the end of the year and so buys one call option outright. We consider two different scenarios.

Stock Price Falling

If the price falls over the course of the year the options will expire worthless. A, who has a short position in the option, will show a profit. A falling price will mean that the long stock hedge will show a loss. As the price falls the stock will be gradually sold resulting in (smaller) additional losses. At the end of the year, B will record a loss. C will also record a loss.

Stock Price Rising

If the price rises sufficiently over the course of the year the options will become in-the-money and A will record a loss. With rising prices, B will record a profit and this profit will increase as more stock is added on the way up. C will also record a profit.

Whatever happens, the total profit to the hedged portfolio will be the sum of managers A and B's profits and losses. If we assume that the actual volatility of the stock price over the year is exactly 15%, the hedged portfolio should break even, whatever the final stock price. To break even the losses on one side of the portfolio must exactly equal the profits on the other.

Let us consider a situation in which the stock price moves with a volatility of 15% but eventually ends the year up at $110. A, who sold the option originally at $5.46, will have to buy it back at $10 and thus record a loss of $100 \times (10 - 5.46) = \$454$. The total hedged portfolio breaks even so B must record a profit of $454 and this is made up of all the profits on the various quantities of long stock acquired over the life of the option. Manager C who simply bought the original option at $5.46 in the hope that the market would rise would record a profit of $100 \times (10 - 5.46) = \$454$— exactly the same as that recorded by B.

Now consider a situation in which the stock price moves with a volatility of 15% but eventually ends the year down at $90. The option will expire worthless. A, who sold the option originally at $5.46, will thus record a profit of $100 \times (5.46 - 0) = \$546$. The total hedged portfolio breaks even so B must record a loss of $546 and this is made up of all the losses on the various quantities of long stock over the life of the option. Manager C will lose his entire stake, i.e. $100 \times 5.46 = \$546$— exactly the same as that recorded by B.

This similarity in the profits and losses of B and C is no coincidence when one thinks of the three individuals in a slightly different way. One can think of a direct link between A and C. A is short one option and C is long the same option. If A and C were to jointly manage a fund, the end result would have been the same—break even. A and C would have equal and opposite positions in the same instrument and so the total fund would be completely neutral. And that is what B is trying to do. B is attempting, via his dynamic hedging activity, to completely neutralise the profits or losses of the short call option. B is attempting to dynamically generate a neutralising long call option position. We can consider B's portfolio as essentially being a synthetic long call option. The dynamic hedging of a short call option in a delta neutral portfolio essentially generates a long call option position. And this is done only with stock. We see that one does not really need an exchange traded options market—we can synthesise options by **dynamic replication**.

There is one important additional point to make. In the above we assumed that whatever the final stock price, the volatility experienced was always 15%. What if the volatility over the life of the option was different from 15%? If the actual volatility experienced is lower (higher) than 15% then the jointly managed short volatility portfolio would produce a profit (loss). Say the actual volatility over the life of the option turns out only to be 10%. At 10% the initial price of the option should have been $3.49, i.e. 5.46 − 3.49 = $1.97 lower than the option priced at 15%. This difference in price of $1.97 or $197 in value, will be the overall total profit jointly recorded by A and B. The pair shorted volatility at 15% and actually experienced only 10%. In this situation even if the stock price ends the year up at $110, the total portfolio profit will still be $197. At $110, A will still have lost 10 − 5.46 = $4.54 per share or $454 as before but to make a net overall profit of $197, B must have made a profit of 454 + 197 = $651. The role of B is exactly the same as before, i.e. one of synthesising a long call option but this time the profit is higher because the volatility was lower. It is as if B has synthesised the call option at a lower price—a price implied by the actual volatility experienced—10%. Synthesising a call option at a lower price has resulted in a larger profit. And that is the fascinating aspect of synthesising options by dynamically trading stock. The price you pay for an option is a direct function of the volatility experienced over the life of the option. This can be completely different from the price you pay when one buys an exchange traded options contract. With an exchange traded option the price you pay is the **expected future volatility**. When you dynamically synthesise an option, the price you pay is a function of the **actual future volatility**.

In the last example we assumed that the real volatility turned out to be lower at 10%. One can follow the same argument for a situation when the real volatility turns out to be higher at say, 20%. At 20%, the option should be worth $7.44, i.e. $1.98 per share more than at 15%. At a volatility of 20%, the portfolio would lose 100 × 1.98 = $198 and this will be because, whatever the final stock price, the cost of synthesising the long call option will be $198 greater than expected.

The above argument shows how it is possible to synthesise a long call option. You start by establishing a long position in the stock. If the price rises you buy more stock and if the price falls you sell stock. At the end of the designated period, the profits or losses to the stock portfolio will be equal to the profits or losses that would have been realised if you had simply bought a call option. The cost of the synthetic call option will not be known until the end of the period. If the stock volatility was particularly low then the option cost will be low. If the stock volatility was high then the cost will be high.

It should be clear that if one reversed the initial positions of A, B and C above, one could just as easily discuss the generation of a short call option. Similarly, it is possible to synthesise a long or short put option by the same process. Synthesising put options became very fashionable in the 1980s. The technique was known as **portfolio insurance**. Exchange traded markets offered only a limited number of options on a limited number of stocks and the portfolio insurance industry capitalised on this by offering put options with any desired expiry date on any portfolio of stocks. One of the really powerful selling points of portfolio insurance was that of costs. In very quiet markets, the cost of synthetically generating puts can be very low. An extreme example is that of one in which the stock price stays completely unchanged over the entire period. Short puts are generated by initially establishing a short stock or stock index future position. In all the examples we consider in this book we have assumed for simplicity that interest rates are zero. In practice they are always of course non-zero. In a non-zero interest rate environment shorting stock produces interest income. So it is possible to imagine a situation in which the synthetic stock put option actually has a negative cost—an extremely attractive proposition indeed. If the stock price is completely stagnant over the life of the synthetic option there will be no trading and hence no trading losses. No trading losses imply that the put option eventually costs nothing. If the short stock position earns interest then the put option actually contributes a net profit rather than a net cost.

The stock market crash of 1987 showed some of the flaws in the concept of portfolio insurance. A dynamically synthesised put option requires the sale of more stock (or stock index futures) as the price falls. In the crash the market was falling so fast that more and more synthetic put program trades triggered more and more sell orders—driving the market down even further. The problem became one of execution. Prices were moving so fast that eventually it became impossible to trade. Some market participants blame the entire crash on the portfolio insurance industry.

We return to the issue of managing complex portfolios of options like those of combinations #1 to #4. If the portfolio is kept delta neutral with long or short stock then what the manager is really doing is synthesising the reverse options portfolio. The simplest of the portfolios, combination #1—the vertical call spread, has one long call position and one short call position. At some stock prices the curvature is negative and at others the curvature is positive. Keeping such a combination delta neutral requires selling stock into a rising market at certain prices and selling stock into a falling market at other prices. If one separates the stock transactions from the rest of the portfolio it becomes clear that all one is doing is dynamically generating the reverse call spread. And the same is true of much more complex portfolios like combination #4. Option fund managers, option market makers and volatility players in general, are all involved in the business of synthesising option portfolios with dynamic stock transactions.

8
More Complex
Aspects of Volatility Trading

In Chapter 3 we introduced the concept of option price curvature. Using a naïve discrete distribution it was possible to show that the price of an option prior to expiry was curved and that this curvature was simply due to the fact that the expiring price profile was kinked. It is clear that whatever assumptions one makes about the stock price distribution, the price profile will always be curved. Also whatever the distribution, if the volatility is high then the option price should ride along a higher curve and all the comments made in Chapter 4 about the effects of volatility on the delta, gamma and theta will still be valid. The Black and Scholes model makes the assumption that the underlying distribution is lognormal. Whether this assumption is valid or not is still the subject of debate. Empirical research shows that provided the period examined is not too long then the lognormal distribution could be a good approximation to the real underlying process. The model also assumes that the volatility of the stock price process is constant and this is often not the case. Stock prices go through volatile periods and quiet periods. Some research suggests that the volatility follows a mean reverting process, i.e. that volatility fluctuates around some long-term average volatility. So can one still use the model to trade volatility or to assess the general risk in an options portfolio? The answer is yes. Fortunately the model is quite robust to the underlying distributional assumptions. In this chapter we address the implications of these and other practical considerations on option pricing.

8.1 TRADING MISPRICED OPTIONS

One of the main reasons for being involved in volatility trading is because one believes that the market has mispriced one or more options. If options are offered at an implied volatility of 15% and a manager believes that the real volatility is now, or is going to be in the future, higher at say 25% then he would set up a long volatility delta neutral portfolio. If the manager's prediction should prove correct then he should profit in one of two ways. The first and simplest way is that he gets lucky in that the rest of the market-place all begin to agree with him and the option price is marked up to that implying a volatility of 25%. If this happens he can unwind the portfolio with a profit. The second way is that in which the market does not agree with him but continues to price the option at an implied volatility of 15% when the underlying volatility is really 25%. If he keeps the portfolio delta neutral by continually trading the underlying, his rehedging profits will exceed the time decay losses with the net result being the same—an overall profit. If transaction costs are very small, the profits will be identical either way.

To keep market neutral requires the accurate estimate of the delta at all stock prices and times to expiry. The Black and Scholes model gives the delta but requires the volatility as an input. Which one do we use—15%, the one the market is pricing the option at, or 25%, the real underlying volatility? In most circumstances the correct input to use would be 15%. If the market is going to continue to price the option at a 15% implied, then as the underlying price changes, the option price will move up and down a curve dictated by using 15%. The fact that the real volatility is 25% is in a way irrelevant. The delta given by using the market implied volatility will ensure that the price changes will be accurately predicted. The fact that the actual volatility is 25% simply means that rehedging occurs more frequently than is necessary.

There are situations when one would not follow the above advice but the correct procedure is not so straightforward and requires some degree of subjectivity. One such situation is immediately after an extraordinary price move. Examples are the US and UK 1987 stock market crashes, the 1990 Japanese stock market crash and the 1992 ERM crisis in the UK interest rate markets. In the 1987 stock market crash some US stock prices fell over 25%. Individuals' short volatility were wiped out and were forced to buy back short option positions at any price. The implied volatility of some stock options soared. Most stock call options that were in-the-money one day were very far out-of-the-money the next day. Usually out-of-the-money call options have very low deltas. However (as noted in Chapter 4) with out-of-the-money call options, if a very high volatility is input into the model, much higher deltas result. In many cases after an extraordinary price move the implied volatility of options increases and then gradually begins to subside back to some lower level. If this happens, using the deltas given by high volatility inputs is inappropriate. The trader needs to make a subjective judgement on the likelihood of the market calming down again. If this happens the price curve will fall back to former levels with the resultant fall in deltas. In the 1987 stock market crash, the volatilities returned to normal levels after three or four weeks, in the 1992 ERM interest rate turmoil it was all over in one week but in the 1990 Japanese stock index options market, it took two years for implied volatilities to return to former levels.

8.2   TRADING PERMANENTLY MISPRICED OPTIONS—EMPIRICAL DELTAS

In the past there have been markets offering permanently mispriced derivative products. These markets provided the opportunity to make large profits. One of the best examples was that of the Japanese warrant market in the period 1987–93. Japanese warrants are very long-dated call options and for various reasons, traded at permanent discounts to the theoretical values given by the Black and Scholes model. At the time, this discrepancy was conveniently explained away by everyone agreeing that the model did not apply to options with lives of four or five years. The main participants in the market were speculators and these were rarely interested in (or understood) theoretical values, deltas or gammas. You just bought the warrants because the market was going up. The liquidity in these instruments was huge in comparison to that in any other equity option market and it was often possible to buy up to $20 million worth of warrants in one day. The large speculative interest and the absence of any significant hedging activity meant that enormous anomalies arose and persisted for years. The most notably mispricing was that which occurred when warrants went in-the-money. Speculators would buy very out-of-the-money warrants at any price, driving up the implied volatility to as high as 40%. If they got lucky, and in the late 1980s they often did, the underlying stock price would rise, driving up the price of the warrant often to five or six times that originally paid. Happy with such large returns, the speculators would then sell in size, often forcing the price to a discount to parity and a large discount to theoretical values. The prices of these in-the-money warrants were often lower than that obtained from the models using zero volatility as an input. These instruments provided hedgers with the opportunity to set up long volatility portfolios at negative costs and this meant that even if the worst case scenario of zero volatility occurred, a profit would still result. And all this was on offer when the Japanese equity market was going through one of its most volatile periods in history.

Some hedgers, however, lost fortunes and this was mainly due to using the wrong deltas. Although everyone agreed that the model gave the wrong prices they happily used the model deltas when setting up portfolios. A typical example would be as follows. With the stock price = 1,000 yen, the exercise price = 1,000 yen and the time to expiry = 4 years, the warrant price in the market would be = 170 yen. At the time, interest rates were approximately 4% and a conservative estimate of stock volatility would be 20%. Substituting these into the standard model and ignoring the effects of stock dividends (which are essentially zero in Japan anyway) would give a theoretical value of 230 yen and a delta of 73%. This example shows the warrant at a 25% discount to the theoretical value, not untypical at the time. Hedgers would buy the warrant and sell 73% of the underlying and wait for a move. The problem was that the actual delta always turned out to be less than the theoretical one. For the warrant in question a typical delta would be 45% not 73%. This invariably meant that the portfolio was net short of the market instead of neutral. In rising markets the portfolios showed very large losses. Figure 8.1 shows the actual market price profile and the theoretical price profile of a typical four year Japanese warrant during the period in question.

Strangely enough institutions such as market makers, involved in the buying and selling of warrants but completely ignorant of such sophisticated models, had a very good feel for the real sensitivities of warrant prices and when setting up hedges used the correct **empirical deltas**. These institutions generated large profits without really knowing why. Over time more and more sophisticated hedgers became involved in the market and used empirical statistical analysis rather

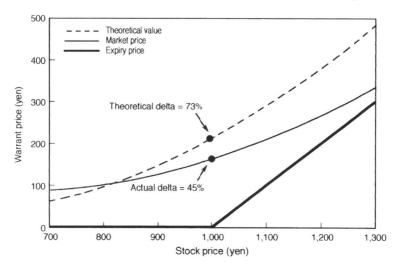

Figure 8.1   Using empirical deltas for Japanese warrants

than Black and Scholes models to estimate deltas. The net effect of all
this hedging activity meant that, unfortunately, the anomalies eventually disappeared. Japanese warrants now trade at prices very near
those given by the model.

8.3   DIFFERENT VOLATILITIES FOR DIFFERENT STRIKE PRICES

The problem with buying volatility low is that one may experience
even lower volatility and that selling volatility high one may experience even higher volatility. Unless the low is extremely low (or in the
case of Japanese warrants, zero) or the high is extremely high there
is no way of guaranteeing a profit. There are occasions when it is
possible to simultaneously buy volatility low and sell volatility high on
the same instrument. In such situations, whatever the actual volatility
a profit results. Consider the following as an extreme example. A
certain stock is trading at $100. There exist two, one-year call options,
with strike prices of $100 and $110 priced at $5.98 and $5.04 respectively. These prices imply volatilities of 15% and 22% respectively.
There is clearly something wrong here. Both options are exercisable
into the common underlying stock and so both should imply the same

volatility. If this situation were to exist in reality a trader would construct a portfolio long of the (cheap) $100 strike option and short of the (expensive) $110 strike option in an attempt to capitalise on the difference in the two prices. The portfolio would be the vertical call spread or combination #1 discussed in Chapter 7. The combination has long exposure and would be hedged with short stock. The rationale behind this strategy is that whatever the true volatility of the stock, buying at 15% and selling at 22% will result in an arbitrage profit. This profit may materialise in one of two ways. One way would be that the market-place suddenly adjusted the option prices so that both have the same (new) implied volatility. For example, if the market adjusted both options to have implied volatilities of 20% the prices would be $7.97 and $4.29 respectively and a profit of $100 \times (7.97 - 5.98 + 5.04 - 4.29) = \$274$ would result. Another way may be that the position is run to expiry with continual dynamic hedging. Whatever the final volatility, the profit (in theory) should be and often will be similar, but because hedging costs are not zero, the final profit will usually be smaller. However, even in this situation a profit is not always guaranteed. It is possible to think of a number of very contrived stock price paths that result in a loss. The simplest one is that of the stock price staying completely fixed at $100 whereupon both options would expire worthless resulting in a loss of $100 \times (5.98 - 5.04) = \$96$.

In the example above the simultaneous buying of volatility at 15% and selling at 22% would most probably result in a profit, but what if the implied volatilities were nearer at say 15 and 17% respectively? Here, we most certainly could not guarantee a profit. In most exchange traded markets it is not uncommon to find options in the same expiry cycles with different strike prices having differing implied volatilities. Initially many practitioners observing such differences put on hedged positions such as the one described above. In the early stages of exchanged traded options markets when the anomalies were large, many of these positions produced profits but some produced losses. Over time, the magnitude of the anomalies have reduced, but they are still there. Some practitioners say that the model is wrong and that implied volatility is not a valid measure of value. Others say that the assumption of a lognormal distribution is not valid and research in this area is ongoing. However, some academics have shown that the anomalies can be explained by relaxing the constant volatility assumption. Almost everyone agrees that volatility varies and that in some markets is related to the price of the underlying. When stock prices fall (rise) there is often an increase (decrease) in volatility. It has been shown that incorporating these and other aspects into the Black and Scholes model would be consistent with different strike prices having different implied volatilities. So the model can still be used but one needs to input different volatilities. Most market participants follow this practice.

The way in which the implied volatilities vary across strike prices depends on the market and market conditions. Stock options typically have higher volatilities at lower strikes and lower volatilities at higher strikes. The standard reasoning behind this type of volatility profile is that in a falling market everyone needs out-of-the-money puts for insurance and will pay a higher price for the lower strike options. Also equity fund managers round the world are long billions of dollars worth of stock and like writing (selling) out-of-the-money call options against their holdings as a way of generating extra income. It is believed that this large scale selling of options has the effect of lowering the implied volatilities of higher strikes. Figure 8.2 shows a graph of such volatilities versus strike prices and this is referred to as a **volatility profile** or **volatility skew**. Practitioners refer to this particular profile as a **volatility smirk**.

Other markets such as options on commodities and commodity futures sometimes have a **reverse volatility smirk** profile. This profile that places higher volatility on higher strikes and lower volatility on lower strikes is sometimes explained by a combination of government intervention and the risk of shortages. In certain commodity markets

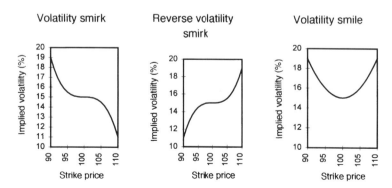

Figure 8.2   Volatility profiles

such as soyabeans there is an unspoken belief that the government will always support the farmer and not let the price fall too low. If the government is going to support a market then there may be no need to worry about a large price fall. Believing this, some speculators are tempted to sell aggressively puts with the result that prices and hence implied volatilities fall. At the other extreme, there are from time to time unforeseen factors that will result in supply shortages and since, in theory, there is no upper limit on the price of a commodity, individuals are prepared to pay up for short cover insurance. The history of commodity markets is littered with examples of extremely violent up moves and it is easy to understand the demand for higher strike price options.

Some markets, such as interest rate options, display what is known as a **volatility smile**. This is where the at-the-money option has a low volatility and either side the volatility is higher. One explanation for this is that individuals have a propensity to sell at-the-money options and buy out-of-the-money options. A popular strategy known as the **Butterfly** involves selling two at-the-money options, hedged with the purchase of one out-of-the-money option and one in-the-money option. This and other similar strategies are low risk and result in maximum pay-off if the options expire with the underlying exactly at the middle strike price.

Whatever the reason, options with different strike prices often have different implied volatilities and this should be incorporated in any risk-monitoring exercise. The software supplied with this book gives the user the ability to input a different volatility for each strike price. Figure 8.3 shows one aspect of the effects of using different volatility profiles with the complex combination #4 discussed in Chapter 7.

8.4 DIFFERENT VOLATILITIES ACROSS TIME

Most stocks options series will have at least three different expiry cycles. Three, six and nine months are the typical expiry cycles. From the discussion of section 8.3 it should be no surprise that the volatilities implied by option prices with different expiry times also differ. As with the differences across strike prices, the differences over expiry cycles are always a function of supply and demand. When markets are very quiet, the implied volatilities of the near month options are generally lower than those of the far month and when markets are

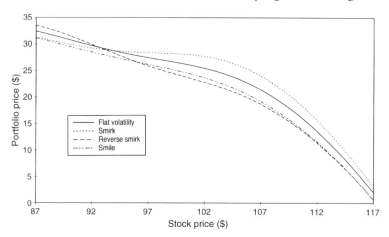

Figure 8.3 Combination #4 with different volatility profiles (90 days to expiry)

very volatile, the reverse is generally true. In quiet markets, option players often get lulled into believing that the quiet times will persist. In quiet markets no one wants a portfolio long of near-dated options and so selling is often the best strategy. Selling in any significant size will drive the price (and the implied volatility) of the near-dated options down. In very volatile markets, everyone wants or needs to load up with gamma. Near-dated options provide the most gamma and the resultant buying pressure will have the effect of pushing prices (and the implied volatilities) up.

Managing a complex options portfolio thus requires the use of a two-dimensional implied volatility matrix. One dimension is across strike prices and the other is across time. The individual volatilities used should reflect, as near as possible, the prices of the options in the market-place. As time passes the structure of the implied volatility matrix may change and this is yet another source of uncertainty that has to be considered.

8.5 FLOATING VOLATILITIES

Some option players believe that the volatility matrix should be dynamic and use what are known as floating volatilities. The idea is that whatever the volatility skew, it should move with the price of the underlying. In this way the at-the-money option will always have the

same volatility but the skew will persist. To illustrate the concept consider a series of stock options that have a volatility smile. Assume that
the central (lowest) value is 15% and that in-the-money and out-of-
the-money options have volatilities that increase uniformly above
15%. As the stock price moves, the entire skewed profile also moves.
Figure 8.4 shows how the volatility profile varies with the stock price.
The rationale behind this type of dynamic skew is that as the underlying price moves what was the out-of-the-money option now becomes
the in-the-money option and some market participants will view the
situation afresh putting the same skew on the new series of prices. If
the market is generally a seller of the at-the-money options then this
will have a lower volatility than the other options. If the underlying
price moves then the new at-the-money option will also be sold. The
problem with this type of dynamic skew is that of estimating delta.
Consider the $95 strike call option. With the stock price at $95 the
volatility input would be 15%. With the stock price up at $105 the $95
strike is now out-of-the-money and has a new volatility of 19%. With
the stock price at values between $95 and $105 the volatility will vary
according to the floating skew to some value between 15 and 19%.
Figure 8.5 gives the price curves of the one option using the two
extreme volatilities. If a floating smile skew is used, the volatility will
vary uniformly between the two extremes and the resultant option
price is also shown. It should be clear that slope of the floating skew
option profile will not be given by using 15 or 19% or any value in

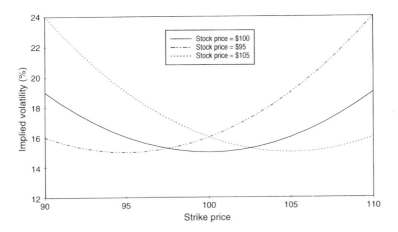

Figure 8.4   Floating volatility smile

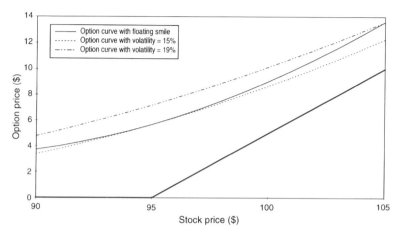

Figure 8.5 Price of $95 call with floating smile

between. Calculating the delta of such an option will not be straight-forward.

Using fixed or floating volatility matrices as described above are attempts by market practitioners to match up the real option prices with those given by the Black and Scholes model. However, whatever the situation, it will always be possible to come up with a volatility that when input into the model gives a price that agrees with the market. But this is not necessarily much use unless we can also arrive at an accurate estimate of the option sensitivities. Using variable or floating volatilities will give accurate option prices but inaccurate deltas.

Different option players use different techniques in managing their portfolios and all agree that there is no one correct method for all markets. Really experienced traders often override model deltas with subjective estimates. If an individual is long a given option and believes that the market will price it at a lower volatility at a higher stock price then he may adjust the delta downwards. If the model tells him that the delta is 0.50, he may use 0.45 instead.

8.6   THE EFFECTS OF TRANSACTION COSTS

Throughout this book we have continually referred to stock options to explain the idea of trading volatility. Stock options were chosen for their implicit simplicity and the fact that they have been around the longest. There are now options on stock indexes, currencies, commodities and bonds. But probably the largest growth has been in futures options markets. There are options on stock index futures, currency futures, commodity futures and interest rate futures. It is not necessary here to go into the details of futures or options on futures and the interested reader is referred to the many excellent texts on the subject. The important point to note is that the options follow the same type of price curves discussed above. The real difference, however, between stock options and futures options is that of transaction costs.

When discussing the long or short volatility portfolios we left the question of transaction costs aside. We either ignored the costs or assumed that they were small. In reality this is sometimes not the case. In some stock markets the cost of dealing in the underlying can be non-trivial and this has implications for the volatility player. If the transaction costs associated with buying or selling the underlying are significant, then the volatility player must incorporate this into his rehedging strategy. If the costs are very high then the long volatility player must wait for a much larger move before rehedging.

The real virtue of trading volatility using options on futures is that the costs, in comparison to those of stocks, are extremely small. As an example, the bid to offer spread on the S&P 500 stock index future is typically 0.02%. Each time a hedger buys or sells a future he is paying away 0.02% of the underlying exposure. The same cost on say IBM stock would be 0.5% and on a typical UK stock such as BP may be as high as 2%. Transaction costs are usually a direct function of the liquidity and most stock index futures contracts are extremely liquid.

8.7 ARBITRAGES BETWEEN DIFFERENT OPTIONS MARKETS

From time to time situations arise that allow the volatility player to profit whatever the underlying market is doing. Because more and more individuals are looking at the derivative markets for these situations they are increasingly difficult to find, but they still do turn up. There are a number of markets where options on the same or a similar product are priced differently. Arbitrageurs typically buy cheap volatility in one market and simultaneously sell expensive volatility in the other.

Options on Stock Indexes versus Options on Stock Index Futures

In the USA there are a number of stock index related options. By far
the largest are the options on the S&P 100 stock index and the options
on the S&P 500 stock index futures contract. The two underlying
stock indexes are highly (but not perfectly) correlated. Even when the
two indexes are not perfectly correlated, the volatilities are usually
very similar. This similarity in volatilities should be, and usually is,
reflected in the relevant option prices. Occasionally, however, the
implied volatilities in one market get out of line with those in the
other market and when this occurs, arbitrageurs buy the cheap options
and sell the expensive options.

Stock Index Options versus Individual Stock Options

Investing in a basket of stocks is, by definition, less risky than investing in an individual stock. The concept of portfolio diversification is
well known. For risk we can of course read volatility and so one would
expect the implied volatilities of stock index options to be lower than
those of an individual stock option. This is indeed the situation in
most markets. Furthermore, there is a well-defined mathematical relationship between the volatility of an index and the individual volatilities of the index constituents but occasionally this relationship is
broken. There occurs from time to time arbitrage opportunities when
the stock index option implied volatilities get out of line with those of
the individual stock option implied volatilities. These situations often
occur in times of extreme market moves. In the 1987 stock market
crash, the UK FTSE index options became extremely expensive as did
the individual stock options. Although high, many of the individual
options were priced the same as the index options and this was clearly
an anomalous situation. Arbitrageurs purchased baskets of individual
stock options and sold short index options. Within three weeks the
portfolios were unwound with large profits.

There are of course other risks in this strategy, the most obvious
one being that the basket of stocks underlying the individual options is
not a match for the index. The FTSE stock index has 100 constituents
and only 60 of these have stock options. The arbitrage trade should
only be instigated when the anomalous option pricing is large enough
to cover any losses associated with mistracking the index.

Japanese Warrants versus Japanese Stock Index Futures

In section 8.2 we mentioned the large profits made, until recently, in the Japanese warrant market. Eventually, more and more hedgers discovered the anomalous price behaviour and everyone got involved in the business of borrowing stock for short selling. Selling stock short is a much more complicated business in Japan than other developed markets. One complication is that associated with stock registration. Most Japanese stock holders have to register details of ownership to the Japanese Ministry of Finance at least once a year and in some cases twice a year. This meant that many volatility players long a warrant and short the underlying were often forced to unwind the trade in order to return stock to the owners for registration. These and other complications made life difficult for the warrant hedger. In fact many market participants believe that these very complications were responsible for the initial abundance of cheap warrants. Over time hedgers gradually found ways round these difficulties and managed to establish long-term agreements with stock-borrowing institutions. These agreements removed the need to periodically unwind trades and so successful hedges could be run for a full four or five years until warrant expiry.

However, there still existed a very large pool of warrants whose underlying stock was impossible to borrow. These warrants could not be hedged and not surprisingly, were the cheapest in the market. The advent of a liquid Japanese stock index futures market in the late 1980s changed the situation. More sophisticated hedgers managed to construct portfolios consisting solely of cheap warrants hedged with short stock index futures contracts. Using sophisticated statistical techniques, they derived special subsets of stocks underlying the cheap warrants that would track the relevant stock index. In this way the hedgers got around the short stock problem completely. In addition to establishing a good market hedge, there were a number of other advantages in using the stock index futures contract. As mentioned before, the costs of dealing in futures are very small and offered a considerable advantage over dealing in stock. Liquidity was another major advantage. Many of the stocks underlying the cheap warrants were almost completely illiquid, whereas the Japanese stock index futures market become one of the most liquid in the world. The profits to the hedgers using stock index futures were enormous, but like everything else, the opportunity only lasted three to four years.

8.8 CONCLUDING REMARKS

In this book we have attempted to explain the idea behind volatility trading. It is possible to construct a portfolio that will benefit or suffer from the volatility, or the lack of volatility, in the price of something. And it is all possible because of the existence of instruments (options) that have a discontinuous, but linear, price profile some time in the future. The fact that, in the future, an option may be worth something or may be worth nothing, and that just one price delineates the boundary between these two states, gives rise to the current price being curved. A curved price profile gives rise to a constantly changing exposure to whatever underlies the option and it is this that enables one to trade volatility. When one is trading a large options portfolio it is sometimes easy to forget that the ever-changing parameters such as the price, the delta, the gamma, the theta and the vega all arise out of a set of discontinuities in the future. We know for certain that in the future, when the options expire, the price of the underlying on that day will make some options worth something and others worth nothing. The fact that we do not know what the exact price of the underlying will be on that day gives rise to the current curvature.

A complete industry (the exchange traded options market) has been built up around instruments that have a future discontinuity. Fortunes have been made and lost on the simple fact that it is difficult to work out today, the current value of a discontinuity in the future. The value is, of course, a direct function of the future volatility of the price of the underlying.

APPENDIX   The Software

The discs supplied with this book contain three programs that should prove useful to the novice and the experienced trader. It is assumed that the reader has little or no experience in programming and so the software is written as a Microsoft Excel spreadsheet. The code has been kept simple and someone with only a rudimentary knowledge of spreadsheets will have little trouble in using and adapting the software. There are no macros and no use of the more complex aspects of Microsoft Excel. Not using the more sophisticated aspects of the spreadsheet package means that the run times may be considered slow by comparison to proprietary risk software. Readers with sufficient programming experience will immediately see how to streamline some of the procedures by use of macros. Most of the tables and graphs displayed in this book were generated using the supplied software.

OPTIONS.XLS

This spreadsheet is the simplest and probably the most useful. It can be used to calculate one-off option values, deltas, gammas, thetas and vegas. Using the in-built Excel What-if problem solver, it is also possible to calculate the implied volatility of an option. The in-built Excel One-input and Two-input Data Table Solver enables multiple option parameters to be calculated and the results graphed. This simple spreadsheet can be used to demonstrate all the complex characteristics of put and call options covered in this book and many not mentioned at all. Much experience on how options behave can be gained by spending time trying various different input values and plotting the resultant output values. Outlined below is a brief description of the spreadsheet entries and the mathematics. The example values given below relate to the option used throughout this book, i.e. the one year at-the-money call option with a volatility of 15% in a zero interest rate environment.

Input variables	Name in spreadsheet	Example value		Cell address
Stock price	s	$100		C4
Exercise price	e	$100		C5
Volatility	v	0.15	(15%)	C6
Time to expiry	t	1.00	(years)	C7
Interest rate	rate	0.0	(0%)	C8
Vega shift	vdif	0.01	(1%)	F4
Time shift	tdif	$= -1/365$	(1 day)	F5
Stock price shift	gdif	$0.1		F6

Intermediate variables *arg1*, *arg2*, *nd1*, *nd2* and *nd11* are computed from the above input variables using the expressions:

Variable	Value	Cell address
$arg1 = (LN(s/e) + (rate + v*v*0.5)*t)/(v*SQRT(t))$	$= 0.0750$	H4
$arg2 = arg1 - v*SQRT(t)$	$= -0.0750$	I4
$nd1 = NORMSDIST(arg1)$	$= 0.5299$	J4
$nd2 = NORMSDIST(arg2)$	$= 0.4701$	K4
$nd11 = EXP(-arg1*arg1*0.5)/SQRT(2*PI())$	$= 0.3978$	L4

The NORMSDIST( ) function returns the cumulative normal distribution value and the result is a number between zero and one. The PI( ) function returns the mathematical constant. LN( ) returns the natural logarithm, EXP( ) returns the exponential number raised to the power of the argument and SQRT( ) returns the square root.

The **Call Option** output variables and example values are given by

Variable	Value	Cell address
call price $= s*nd1 - e*EXP(-rate*t)*nd2$	$= 5.9785$	C12
call delta $= nd1$	$= 0.5299$	C13
call vega $= s*SQRT(t)*nd11*vdif$	$= 0.3978$	C14
call theta $= tdif*(s*v*nd11/2*SQRT(t))$		
$+ e*rate*EXP(-rate*t)*nd2)$	$= -0.0082$	C15
call del (vega) $= vdif*(-arg2*nd11/v)$	$= 1.989E-03$	C17
call del (theta) $= tdif*nd11*(rate/(v*$		
$SQRT(t)) - arg2/(2*t))$	$= -4.087E-05$	C18
call gamma $= gdif*nd11/(s*v*SQRT(t))$	$= 2.652E-03$	C19

We interpret the output values as follows:

- The **call option price** is $5.98 per share. So if the option is exercisable into 100 shares then one option would cost $598.
- The **call delta** is 0.53. A small change in the underlying stock price will alter the value of the option by 53% of the small change. As an exercise, increase the stock price $0.10 to $100.10 and see the effect on the option

price. The option price should increase by 0.53 × 0.10 = $0.053. The new price is $6.03—exactly as predicted by the delta. This is of course only valid for small stock price changes.

- The **call vega** is 0.40. A small change (given by the vega shift parameter of 1% or 0.01) will alter the price of the option by $0.40 per share. As an exercise, increase the volatility parameter from 15 to 16%. Note that the new option price is $6.38—an increase of exactly $0.40. As with all rates of change, this is only valid for small volatility shifts. In order to find out what effect a dramatic change such as 10% would make, simply change the volatility parameter.
- The **call theta** is −0.0082. The time shift parameter in this example is set to the very small value of 1 day (= 1/365 = 0.00274 of a year). The call theta output value tells us that with the passage of one day, the option will lose $0.0082 per share in value. If the time shift parameter is set to 1 week (= 1/52 = 0.0192 of a year), the theta changes to −0.0574 which is almost exactly seven times the theta due to one day. With one year to expiry the theta decay is almost linear.
- The vega of the delta: **del (vega)** is 0.001989 or 0.002 approximately. If the volatility of the option is increased by the vega shift amount (1% in this example) then the delta of the option increases by 0.002. With the volatility set at 15% the delta is 0.5299 and so 100 options exercisable into 100 shares would be exposed to 100 × 100 × 0.5299 = 5,299 stock units. The change in delta caused by increasing the volatility to 16% would increase the stock exposure by 100 × 100 × 0.002 = 20 stock units to 5,319.
- The theta of the delta **del (theta)** is -0.00004087. The passage of one day reduces the delta of the option by this very small amount.
- The **gamma** is 0.002652. The stock shift input variable is set to $0.10. The gamma output variable gives the change in delta caused by a change in the underlying stock price of $0.10. In this case a portfolio containing 100 options exercisable into 100 shares would have a stock exposure of 5,299 units. If the underlying stock price were to increase from $100.00 to $100.10 then the stock exposure would increase by 100 × 100 × 0.002652 = 26 stock units to 5,325.

The corresponding **Put Option** output variables and example values are calculated from the call option values and are given by

Variable	Value	Cell Address
put price = call price $-s + e * \text{EXP}(-rate * t)$	= 5.9785	G12
put delta = call delta − 1	= −0.4701	G13
put vega = call vega	= 0.3978	G14
put theta = call theta	= −0.0082	G15
put del (vega) = call del (vega)	= 1.989E-03	G17
put del (theta) = call del (vega) $- tdif * e *$ $rate * \text{EXP}(-rate * t)$	= −4.087E-05	G18
put gamma = call gamma	= 2.652E-03	G19

Using the One-input Data Table to Generate Tables and Figures

To see how changes in one variable affect one or more option characteristics, use the One-Input Data Table facility of Microsoft Excel. The example given in the OPTIONS.XLS file shows how to generate Figures 3.7 and 3.8 illustrating how the price and delta of a one year call option vary with respect to the underlying stock price. The data table is set up so that the range J13 . . J25 contains the various stock prices: 70, 75, 80, ..., 130. The K12 and L12 cells contain the formulae: [= call] and [= nd1] respectively. In order to generate a table containing the call price and call delta at each level of stock price one first selects the rectangular range (J12 . . L25). Then choose Table from the Data menu. The input parameter that is to be varied in this example is the stock price and in the main body of the spreadsheet the stock price is input into the Cell C4. Since the actual values of the variable input appear in a column, specify C4 as the Column Input Cell and choose OK. Two columns of values corresponding to call price and call delta appear in the ranges (K13 . . K25) and (L13 . . L25) respectively. Charting the resultant output is straightforward. See Figure A.1 for details.

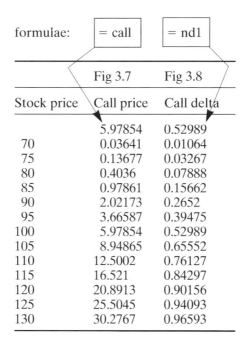

formulae:	= call	= nd1
	Fig 3.7	Fig 3.8
Stock price	Call price	Call delta
	5.97854	0.52989
70	0.03641	0.01064
75	0.13677	0.03267
80	0.4036	0.07888
85	0.97861	0.15662
90	2.02173	0.2652
95	3.66587	0.39475
100	5.97854	0.52989
105	8.94865	0.65552
110	12.5002	0.76127
115	16.521	0.84297
120	20.8913	0.90156
125	25.5045	0.94093
130	30.2767	0.96593

Figure A.1 Using the One-input Data Table to examine the dependence of call price and delta on stock price with volatility, exercise price, time to expiry and interest rate fixed at 15%, $100, 1 year and 0% respectively

It is possible to extend the One-input Data Table facility of Microsoft Excel to include any number of formulae. One could extend the given table to include the output values of vega, theta or gamma to see how these values vary with the underlying stock price.

The tables and figures generated by this method show how an option price, delta, vega, etc. vary with respect to the underlying stock price. It is a simple matter to show how these characteristics vary with respect to any other variable. By placing various values of volatility say 8%, 9%, 10%, ... in the range (J12 .. J25) and specifying the Cell C6 (the input volatility cell) it is possible to see how all the above outputs depend on volatility at a given stock price. Figure A.2 shows how the price, the delta and the gamma of a call option vary with volatility.

Using a similar approach one can examine the dependence of each of the option characteristics on: time to expiry, interest rates and exercise price.

Using the Two-input Data Table to Generate Tables and Figures

To see how changes in two variables affect an option characteristic, use the Two-input Data Table facility of Microsoft Excel. The example given in the OPTIONS.XLS file shows how to generate Figure 4.11 illustrating the time

formulae:	= call	= nd1	= C19
Volatility	**Call price**	**Call delta**	**Call gamma**
	5.97854	0.52989	0.00265215
8%	3.1907	0.51595	0.00498279
9%	3.58928	0.51795	0.00442821
10%	3.98777	0.51994	0.00398444
11%	4.38617	0.52193	0.00362127
12%	4.78445	0.52392	0.00331854
13%	5.18261	0.52591	0.00306231
14%	5.58065	0.5279	0.00284261
15%	5.97854	0.52989	0.00265215
16%	6.37629	0.53188	0.00248542
17%	6.77387	0.53387	0.00233826
18%	7.17129	0.53586	0.00220739
19%	7.56853	0.53784	0.00209024
20%	7.96558	0.53983	0.00198476

Figure A.2   Using the One-input Data Table to examine the dependence of call price, delta and gamma on volatility with stock price, exercise price, time to expiry and interest rate fixed at $100, $100, 1 year and 0% respectively

decay effects on an option price, delta and gamma at various stock prices. The data table is set up in the range (N12 . . S25). The stock prices: 80,84,88, . . . are in the column range (N13 . . N25). The five different times to maturity: 12 months, 6 months, 3 months, 1 month and 1 week are in the row range (O12 . . S12). The N12 Cell contains the formulae: [= call]. First select the data range (N12 . . S25). Then choose Table from the Data menu. The input parameters that are to be varied in this example are the stock price and the time to expiry. In the main body of the spreadsheet the stock price is input into the Cell C4 and the time to expiry is input into Cell C7. Since the variable values of the stock price input appear in a column, specify C4 as the Column Input Cell and since the variable values of the time to expiry input appear in a row, specify C7 as the Row Input Cell. Choose the OK button. A two-dimensional table containing values corresponding to call prices appears. Charting the resultant output to obtain the first display in Figure 4.11 is straightforward. See Figure A.3 for details.

To generate the two-dimensional table of various delta values one simply has to alter the formulae in the formulae cell to [= nd1]. To get the various gamma values change the formulae cell to [= C19].

formulae: | = call |

Stock price	12 months	6 months	3 months	1 month	1 week
5.9785426	1	0.5	0.25	0.083333	0.019231
80	0.403602	0.060652	0.002794	8.93E-08	0
84	0.831189	0.203396	0.023391	2.51E-05	0
88	1.538656	0.551731	0.127214	0.001835	1.19E-10
92	2.601739	1.252073	0.482042	0.042938	1.37E-05
96	4.074152	2.447767	1.355101	0.393674	0.019124
100	5.978543	4.229453	2.991378	1.727344	0.82984
104	8.304948	6.605334	5.458891	4.438762	4.024348
108	11.01658	9.506561	8.617404	8.067986	8.000056
112	14.05905	12.81874	12.22671	12.00635	12
116	17.37077	16.4191	16.07252	16.00036	16
120	20.89127	20.20266	20.02034	20.00001	20
124	24.56681	24.09288	24.00504	24	24
128	28.35309	28.04049	28.00111	28	28

Figure A.3 Using the Two-input Data Table to examine the joint dependence of call price, on stock price and time to expiry with exercise price, volatility and interest rate fixed at $100, 15% and 0% respectively

Finding the Implied Volatility Using the What-if Solver

The theoretical value of an option depends (usually) on five inputs: the stock price, the exercise price, the interest rate, the time to expiry and the volatility parameter. The first four are known and easy to measure. The volatility parameter is unknown and is often estimated using historic analysis. Alternatively one can simply make a subjective guess at what future volatility is likely to be. Substituting the five inputs into the model given in OPTIONS.XLS will give the option price, the delta, etc. It is often useful to ask the reverse question, i.e. if the market price of the option today is such and such what does this imply about the future volatility of the stock? In other words, what volatility input into the model will give a theoretical price that exactly matches the market price—what is the implied volatility of the option?

One solution is to try different volatility values repeatedly in Cell C6 until the theoretical option price (in Cell C12 for call options or Cell G12 for put options) exactly matches the market price. This will work but can be tedious. The real virtue of using Microsoft Excel is that there is a special function that can solve this sort of problem quickly—the **Goal Seek Command**. We have a formula giving the theoretical value of an option in terms of a volatility input. We are in the situation that we know the result of the formula (the market price of the option) but we do not know the input value the formula needs to reach that result. The Goal Seek Command varies the value in a cell you specify until a formula that is dependent on that cell returns the result you want.

In the example in OPTIONS.XLS the formula for the call option is in Cell C12 and the unknown volatility is in Cell C6. Say we wish to find the implied volatility of the one year at-the-money call option if the price is not $5.98 but $7.0. Choose Goal Seek from the Tools menu. In the Set Cell box put C12. In the To Value box put 7.5 (you are setting the formula given in Cell C12 to equal to 7.5). In the By Changing Value box put C6 and choose OK. The result appears quickly as 18.83%. So if a volatility value of 18.83% is input into the model the theoretical option price is $7.5. The implied volatility of the option is 18.83%. It is that simple.

RISK1.XLS

This spreadsheet generates some of the risk matrix outputs shown in Chapter 7. The first of these—Table 7.3—is reproduced here for ease of reference purposes. The file supplied contains exactly the same portfolio, i.e. short 200 three-month $95 strike puts, long 100 three-month $105 strike puts and long 100 six-month $115 strike calls. For simplicity we will use this portfolio to explain all the features of this risk spreadsheet. As will become obvious later,

Table 7.3   Risk statistics: $-200 \times$ (3-month \$95 puts) $+ 100 \times$ (3-month \$105 puts) $+100 \times$ (6-month \$115 calls). (Vol shift = 1%, time shift = 1 day, stock price shift = \$0.10, portfolio value at \$100 = \$45,572)

	Profit and loss (\$)			Equivalent stock position (stock units)			
Stock Price	Profit	Profit (+ vol)	Profit (+ time)	ESP	ESP (+ vol)	ESP (+ time)	Gamma
76	−135,620	−36	+3	+9,970	−20	+2	−2
80	−96,027	−231	+20	+9,977	−90	+8	−10
84	−58,231	−848	+72	+8,970	−222	+19	−33
88	−25,923	−1,904	+164	+6,945	−273	+24	−69
92	−4,396	−2,656	+235	+3,673	−54	+7	−90
96	+3,302	−2,089	+203	+300	+341	−23	−72
100	**0**	**−144**	**+65**	**−1,611**	**+582**	**−42**	**−21**
104	−6,707	+2,132	−95	−1,409	+508	−35	+29
108	−9,186	+3,682	−196	+343	+256	−15	+55
112	−3,260	+4,215	−221	+2,636	+25	+1	+57
116	**+11,649**	**+4,017**	**−198**	**+4,755**	**−107**	**+9**	**+48**
120	+34,182	+3,463	−160	+6,432	−160	+10	+36
124	+62,511	+2,788	−122	+7,664	−172	+9	+26

we can expand the position to contain options with up to nine different strike prices and three different expiry cycles. The experienced programmer will also be able to amend the file to increase the number of strikes and expiry cycles.

The spreadsheet is organised in 14 different sheets. The front or first sheet contains all the input data and the output risk matrix given above. The mathematical computations are carried out on each of the other 13 sheets. Each of the 13 different sheets contains information relating to the 13 rows of Table 7.3 and each of the 13 rows corresponds to a different possible stock price. The 13 sheets (Sheet 3, sheet 4, ..., Sheet 15) contain exactly the same formulae. The sheets only differ in that the entry in the Cell B1 is a stock price corresponding to those printed in the summary risk matrix. So in the given example, Cell B1 on Sheet 3 contains the stock price 76, the Cell B1 on Sheet 4 contains the stock price 80 and so on until Sheet 15 where Cell B1 contains the stock price of 124. Sheet 2 is left blank. We now consider the front or first sheet—Sheet 1.

Sheet 1. Summary Information and Portfolio Position

The range A1 . . G70 contains much of the basic input data. Some of the input variables are single numbers and many have variable names. Other variables are in the form of vectors or ranges and these are also named.

General Single Number Input Variables

A brief description of each of the single number input variables is listed below along with each variable's cell address, name and example values.

- **Cell B3** (*smid*) is the central stock price that appears in the computed risk matrix output. It usually makes sense to pick the current stock price as the central price. The output table thus shows the various risk characteristics at stock prices around this central value. In the given example this value is set to 100.
- **Cell D3** (*sdif*) is the price difference. This value dictates the range of different stock prices used in producing the risk matrix. In the given example the value is set to 4 so that the difference between each successive stock price is $4. Thus the 13 different stock prices: $76, $80, $84, ... , $124 are calculated using: $(smid - 6 * sdif)$, $(smid - 5 * sdif)$, $(smid - 4 * sdif)$, ... , $(smid + 6 * sdif)$.
- **Cell D1** has the function TODAY() which returns the current date in the relevant format. This is used in calculating the time to expiry of the various options.
- **Cell D2** (*rate*) is the relevant interest rate. In the given example this is set to zero.
- **Cell D4** is the theta difference parameter in days. In the given example this value is set to 1 day and so the output values in the columns headed (+ time) represent the change in P&L or delta caused by the passing of 1 day.
- **Cell F4** (*tdif*) is the theta difference parameter that is used in all subsequent mathematical computations. Accordingly it is expressed in years and is given a minus sign. This value is calculated from the entry in Cell D4 using the expression: $[= -D4/365]$.
- **Cell D5** (*vdif*) is the vega difference parameter. In the given example this value is set to 0.01 or 1% and so the output values in the columns headed (+ vol) represent the changes in P&L or delta caused by increasing volatility across the board by 1%.
- **Cell D6** (*gdif*) is the gamma difference parameter and in the given example is set to 0.10. With this setting, the entries in the gamma column of the risk matrix indicate the change in stock exposure caused by an increase in the underlying stock price of $0.10 or 10 cents.
- **Cell D7** (*mult*) is the option multiplier. In the given example this is set to 100 because all options discussed in this book are exercisable into 100 shares. Different options markets have different numbers of shares per option. The UK and Australian stock options contracts, for example, are exercisable into 1,000 shares. Many options on futures contracts are exercisable into just one future.
- **Cell B5** (*ssz*) is the stock position. Often a complex options portfolio will also contain a long or short position in the underlying stock. If the portfolio in question had a short position, say in 5,000 shares, then one should input −5,000 into this cell. In the example given, this cell is set to zero since the portfolio has no stock position.

- **Cell B6** (*spr*) is the average stock price. In the given example this is irrelevant and so is set to zero. However, say the portfolio had a short position in 5,000 shares then the average price of the position should be placed in this cell. As an example, say the share position was acquired as the result of shorting 2,000 shares at $100 and shorting 3,000 shares at $110, then the average share price input into Cell B6 should be

$$spr \begin{aligned} &= \frac{2,000 \times \$100 + 3,000 \times \$110}{5,000} \\ &= \$106 \end{aligned}$$

- **Cell B7** (*scost*) is the cost of carrying the stock position. The cost of carrying a stock position is calculated from the theta difference parameter, the interest rate, the average stock price and the stock position using the following expression:

$$scost = -rate * ssz * spr * tdif$$

In the given example the cost is obviously zero but consider the situation if the portfolio has a short position of 5,000 units at an average cost of $106. If interest rates were 10% and the theta parameter set to 1 day, this means that the cost of running the stock position would be

$$scost = -0.10 * (-5000) * 106 * (1/365) = +\$145.21$$

The position has a net positive cost of carry. The short position is generating an income of $145.21 per day. With large stock positions this cost can have a considerable effect on the (+ time) column in the P&L section of the risk matrix.

Expiry Specific Single Number Input Variables

The example spreadsheet RISK1.XLS has three different expiry cycles situated in the ranges A9 . . G24, A32 . . G47 and A55 . . G70 respectively. The single number input variables associated with the first expiry are as follows:

- **Cell D9** is the expiry date in the correct format for the options in expiry cycle #1.
- **Cell D10** is the number of days to expiry of this cycle and is computed as the difference between Cell D9 and the current date in Cell D1.
- **Cell D11** (*time1*) is the time to expiry of the options in cycle #1 expressed in years and is simply the number of days divided by 365. The variable *time1* is a single number variable that is used throughout the spreadsheet when referring to those positions in cycle #1 options.

Cells in the ranges containing expiry cycle #2 and #3 option positions have similar entries. The single number variables corresponding to the time (in years) to expiry are *time2* and *time3* respectively. In order to replicate exactly the figures in Table 7.3 it will be necessary to alter the expiry dates so that the number of days to expiry are 90, 182 and 272 respectively.

Expiry Specific Range Input Variables or Vectors

To simplify the mathematical expressions the spreadsheet utilises the range variable facility of Microsoft Excel. This allows a column (or row) of numbers to be referred to by a single mathematical expression. The spreadsheet has six such range variables:

● **Range: C16 . . C70** (*exprice*) is the set of exercise prices for all expiry cycles.
● **Range: B16 . . B70** (*vol*) is the set of individual volatilities. In the given example each element is set to 15% but the user can set each volatility to separate values.
● **Range: D16 . . D70** (*putsz*) is the set of put option positions for all expiry cycles and all strike prices. In the given example the portfolio has a short position of 200 options in the near (3-month) $95 strike puts and a long position of 100 puts in the near (3-month) $105 puts. Accordingly the Cell D18 has the entry −200 and the Cell D20 the entry +100 with all other cells set to zero.
● **Range: F16 . . F70** (*callsz*) is the set of call option positions for all expiry cycles and all strike prices. In the given example the portfolio has a long position of 100 options in the mid (6-month) $115 strike calls. Accordingly the Cell F45 has the entry +100 with all other cells set to zero.
● **Range: E16 . . E70** (*putpr*) is for the average executed prices for each put option. These averages are computed in a similar fashion to the average stock price above. In the given example the 3-month $95 and $105 put averages are set to $1.05746 and $6.17616 respectively.
● **Range: G16 . . G70** (*callpr*) is for the average executed prices for each call option. In the given example the 6-month $115 call average is set to $0.49599.

It is not essential to input the last two variables, *putpr* and *callpr*, as these are only used in calculating the P&L column in the final risk matrix. The rest of the risk matrix is completely independent of these prices.

All the information necessary to calculate the risk matrix is on Sheet 1 described above and for the non-mathematician and non-programmer that is all one needs to know. The reader is invited to experiment with the software by constructing various portfolios. The resultant risk matrices can be examined in tabular form or printed in chart form. Those readers not interested in the mathematics of the risk software can skip the next section.

Sheet 3 to Sheet 15   A Description of the Mathematical Procedures

The mathematical computations are carried out on 13 individual sheets: Sheets 3 to 15. The layout of each of these sheets is identical but to illustrate the mathematical procedures in all we will henceforth refer to just one: **Sheet 5**.

Sheet Stock Price

The very first cell in Sheet 5: Cell B1 contains the formula [= *smid* − 4 ∗ *sdif*] and in the given example this becomes: 100 − 4 ∗ 4 = 84. This then is the set price for this sheet and all the risk characteristics will be computed on this value. Eventually the results (just seven totals) will be sent back to the front sheet and be placed in the third row of the risk matrix (the one showing a stock price of $84). This stock price of $84 is used throughout Sheet 5 and so is given the local variable name: *s*.

Option Details

All the range variables relating to the exercise prices, volatilities, position sizes and average execution prices are copied over into the relevant positions. So the cells in the Sheet 5!Range B16 . . B70 all have the formula [= *vol*], all the cells in the Sheet 5!Range C16 . . C70 have the formula [= *exprice*], etc. This is of course unnecessary and does take up extra space; these figures are repeated in each and every one of the 13 sheets. However, as will be discovered below, it is sometimes useful (especially for the novice) to inspect the specific risk characteristics of each individual option at various stock prices. Having the option input variables, such as exercise price and volatility, printed on each sheet can be quite helpful.

All the characteristics of each option position are computed using expressions identical to those given in the spreadsheet OPTIONS.XLS. These include: (i) the theoretical price, (ii) the vega, (iii) the theta, (iv) the delta, (v) the vega of the delta, (vi) the theta of the delta and (vii) the gamma. The calculations require the computation of intermediate variables such as the values of *arg1*, *arg2*, *nd1*, *nd2* and *nd11* and these are carried out in the corresponding rows using expressions involving the range variables. To save space these intermediate variables are not named but are referred to elsewhere using the usual cell references. The first option with a non-zero position is the put with an exercise price of $95. This option resides in the 18th row and the formula corresponding to the intermediate variable *arg1* for this option is

AC18 = (LN(*s*/*exprice*) + (*rate* + 0.5 ∗ *vol* ∗ *vol*) ∗ *time1*)/
(*vol* ∗ SQRT (*time1*)) = −1.61491

This variable is equivalent to the *arg1* variable in OPTIONS.XLS. Here the named variable *s* is local and in Sheet 5 is set to 84. The named variables: *rate* and *time1* are single numbers. The variable *rate* is the one global interest rate (here set to 0%) and the variable *time1* is the time to expiry of the first cycle (= 90/365 years). The range variables: *exprice* and *vol* refer to the vector of exercise prices and associated volatilities. Although the expression has mixed name variables, the virtue of Microsoft Excel is that only the appropriate element is used in the calculation. In the above example the formula is in the 18th row of Sheet 5 and so relevant row elements of the *exprice* and *vol* vector used are 95 and 0.15 respectively. Below are the rest of the mathematical expressions used to calculate each of the intermediate variables for the options in the first expiry cycle. The results of the calculations are also given:

$$AD18 = AC18 - vol * SQRT (time1) = arg2 = -1.68941$$
$$AE18 = NORMSDIST (AC16) = nd1 = 0.05317$$
$$AF18 = NORMSDIST (AD16) = nd2 = 0.04557$$
$$AG18 = EXP (-0.5 * AC16 * AC16)/(SQRT (2 * PI ()))$$
$$= nd11 = 0.10829$$

The option sensitivities are calculated directly from these variable using identical expressions to those given in OPTIONS.XLS.

Theoretical value $= I18 = s * (AE18 - 1) - EXP(-rate * time1)$
$* exprice * (AF18 - 1) = 11.13654$
Delta $= J18 = AE18 - 1 = -0.94684$

So this option at the new stock price of $84 is now worth 11.13654 and has a new delta of −0.94684. This option was originally shorted at a price of 1.05746 when the stock price was $100. This represents a loss of 11.13654 − 1.05746 = $10.07908 per unit of stock. The position size is 200 options with each option exercisable into 100 units of stock and so the total loss is 200 * 100 * 10.07908 = 201,582. The general expression for the P&L on this option sits in Cell K18 and is given by

$$P\&L = K18 = putsz * mult * (I18 - putpr) = -201,582$$

At a stock price of $84 this option has a delta of −0.94684. The portfolio is short this position so the stock exposure will be long 0.94684 per unit. The position size is 200 and so the net stock exposure will be 200 * 100 * 0.94684 = +18,936 units. The general expression for the stock exposure sits in Cell X18 and is given by

$$ESP = N18 = putsz * mult * J18 = +18,936$$

The mathematical expressions, cell references and resultant values of each of the other five sensitivities are as follows:

P&L(+vol) $= L18 = putsz * mult * vdif * s * \text{SQRT}(time1)*AG18 = -903$

P&L(+time) $= M18 = putsz * mult * tdif * (s * vol * AG18/(2 * \text{SQRT}(time1))$
              $+ exprice * rate * (AF18 - 1) * \text{EXP}(-rate * time1)) = +75$

ESP(+vol) $= O18 = putsz * mult * vdif * (-AD18 * AG18/vol) = -244$

ESP(+time) $= P18 = putsz * mult * tdif * (rate\ vol * *\text{SQRT}(time1) -AD18/(2*time1)) = +20$

Gamma $= Q18 = putsz * mult * gdif * AG18/(s * vol * \text{SQRT}(time1)) = -35$

These figures are interpreted as follows:

−903: If volatility increases by *vidf* (1%) then this particular option position will lose a further $903.

+75: If *tdif* days (1 day) pass this particular option will contribute a further profit of $75.

−244: If volatility increases by *vidf* (1%) then the stock exposure of this particular option position will decrease by 244 stock units.

+20: If *tdif* days (1 day) pass then the stock exposure of this particular option position will increase by 20 stock units.

−35: If the underlying stock price increase by *gdif* (0.1) then the stock exposure of this particular option position will decrease by 35 units.

All of the above figures were computed using the entries in the 18th row of Sheet 5. The 18th row contains information relating to the short 200 3-month $95 put options. Examination of the 20th row will show that identical expressions give information on the long 100 3-month $105 put options. The sensitivities relating to call options, in particular the long 100 6-month $115 calls, appear in the 45th row and the columns S45 to AA45. The total P&L and all the sensitivities are simply added together. The seven totals are placed in the Cells K77 to Q77. Table A.1 summarises the risk statistics from Sheet 5 associated with the position with the stock price set to $84.

These final seven totals are then copied back to Sheet 1 to the row containing the stock price of $84. This is done in Sheet 1, Cells I79 to P79 using the formula: [= Sheet 5!$K77, = Sheet 5!$L77, etc.]. There are some additional components to the P&L columns associated with the stock position (if any).

This then is how the entry corresponding to the stock price of $84 is generated. An identical process takes place on each of the sheets but with each sheet having a different value for the local variable: *s*, the stock price. The resultant risk matrix reproduced in Table 7.3 is then a grand summary of the

Table A.1   The risk statistics of combination #3 with the stock price set to $84 (Sheet 5)

Position	Option	Profit	Profit (+ vol)	Profit (+ time)	ESP	ESP (+ vol)	ESP (+ time)	Gamma
−200	3-month $95 puts	−201,582	−903	+75	+18,936	−244	+20	−35
+100	3-month $105 puts	+148,266	+21	−2	−9,985	+10	+−1	+1
+100	6-month $115 calls	−4,915	+34	−2	+18	+12	−1	+1
Total		−58,231	−848	+72	+8,970	−222	+19	−33

overall sensitivities of the portfolio to changes in volatility, time and stock price.

The real virtue of the way in which the spreadsheet has been designed is that, although it is cumbersome and relatively slow, it is possible to examine the breakdown of each individual component. On Sheet 5 for example, with the stock price at $84, the short position in the $95 strike put is clearly the most dominant portion of the portfolio in terms of stock exposure. At this stock price level, this position is contributing +18,936 units of stock exposure and dominates both of the other components. Examination of Sheet 13 reproduced in Table A.2 shows that at a stock price of $116, this stock exposure is reduced considerably to +66 units. At $116 the put has almost no contribution all.

The design of the spreadsheet RISK1.XLS is clearly not optimal. There is much unnecessary duplication and absolutely no use of the very sophisticated macro facility of Microsoft Excel. This was a deliberate decision on the part of the author. Although cumbersome, the spreadsheet in its supplied form, should be easy to follow. However, once understood, even the novice pro-

Table A.2   The risk statistics of combination #3 with the stock price set to $116 (Sheet 13)

Position	Option	Profit	Profit (+ vol)	Profit (+ time)	ESP	ESP (+ vol)	ESP (+ time)	Gamma
−200	3-month $95 puts	+20,973	−114	+10	+66	+35	−3	−2
+100	3-month $105 puts	−58,310	+893	−74	−846	−134	+11	+18
+100	6-month $115 calls	+48,986	+3,238	−133	+5,536	−8	0	+32
Total		+11,649	+4,017	−198	+4,755	−107	+9	+48

grammer should be able to begin trimming the spreadsheet. One suggestion is that the duplication of the range variables: *vol, exprice, putsz, putpr, callsz,* and *callpr* on Sheets 3 to 15 be deleted. A second suggestion is that the sensitivities be carried out using macros.

RISK2.XLS

This spreadsheet generates charts such as that illustrated in Figure 7.12. This spreadsheet is only concerned with calculating the **value** of the given portfolio at various times to expiry and at various stock prices. The example in the supplied file is exactly the same as combination #4 shown in Table 7.10 and is reproduced here.

The spreadsheet is similar to RISK1.XLS in that all the standard information such as stock price, stock price difference, exercise price, volatility, call and put positions appear in exactly the same cells. As with RISK1.XLS the input and resultant output information appear on Sheet 1. Also, as with RISK1.XLS, each of the Sheets 3 to 15 is used to calculate values for each of the different stock prices. In this spreadsheet we are not concerned with the calculation of delta or any of the influences on delta or gamma and we are not interested in the effects of volatility on the P&L of the portfolio. Accordingly this spreadsheet is much less complex than RISK1.XLS.

The output appears in the Range: Sheet 1!H75 . . L89 and is the portfolio value on four different dates. The four different dates are defined by the Cells D4, E4, F4 and G4 in terms of days. The user can alter the values of these cells to see the how time affects the value of the portfolio. In the example supplied, all the options expire in 90 days and the entries in the given cells are 0, 30, 70 and 88 days respectively. With these inputs, the output values will correspond to portfolio valuations at the following number of days left to maturity:

1st P&L column corresponds to: $90 - 0 = 90$ days to expiry
2nd P&L column corresponds to: $90 - 30 = 60$ days to expiry
3rd P&L column corresponds to: $90 - 70 = 20$ days to expiry
4th P&L column corresponds to: $90 - 88 = 2$ days to expiry

Table 7.10 Net option position of combination #4

Strike price	$90	$95	$100	$105	$110	Total
Call position	+3	−4	+3	−1	−4	
Put position	−6	+8	−2	−3	+3	
Net position	**−3**	**+4**	**+1**	**−4**	**−1**	**−3**

The mathematical expressions must have the times to expiry in years and so the *time1* variable is defined as being these values expressed in years. Here the *time1* variable is a range variable not a single number variable. Note also that the *time1* variable has the four different entries repeated three times. This is a device used to make the calculations in Sheets 3 to 15 simpler.

Sheet 3 to Sheet 5   Description of the Mathematical Procedures

As with RISK1.XLS we illustrate the mathematics of Sheets 3 to 15 by referring to a typical example, i.e. **Sheet 5**.

Sheet Stock Price

The Cell Sheet 5!B1 contains the formula [= *smid* − 4 * *sdif*] and in the given example this cell has the value 84.

Option Details

For simplicity, in this spreadsheet, the option details such as *vol, exprice*, etc. are not copied over. In the following mathematical expressions these variables are used but the relevant values are obtained from Sheet 1.

This file is only concerned with the calculation of P&L and therefore is only concerned with the calculation of the theoretical value. To calculate the theoretical values of call and put options one only needs to calculate the values of the variables *nd1* and *nd2* referred to in OPTIONS.XLS and RISK2.XLS. In this spreadsheet these variables are computed using much more comprehensive formula. The 3-month $90 strike put option information is in the 18th row throughout and so in Sheet 5 the value of *nd1* are computed in Cells Sheet 5!N18 . . Q18. Each of the four values corresponding to each of the four different times of expiry. Similarly the Cells Sheet 5!S18 . . V18 contain the values of *nd2*. The theoretical values are calculated from these cell values and appear in Cells Sheet 5!I18 . . L18.

The total theoretical value of the portfolio is simply the sum of the individual theoretical values and these are calculated and placed in Cells Sheet 5!I72 . . L72. These sets of figures represent the value of the portfolio with the stock price set to $84. These final totals are then copied back to Sheet 1 and placed in the Cells Sheet 1!I79 . . L79. There are also some additional commands relating to the stock position (if any).

This then is how the $84 row in the final output table is computed. The process is duplicated for each of the different stock prices dictated by the *smid* and *sdif* variables. The tabulated output corresponding to Figure 7.12 is reproduced in Table A3.

Table A.3 Combination #4 valuation at various times to expiry

Stock price	P&L(time 1)	P&L(time 2)	P&L(time 3)	P&L(time) 4
76	3,493.61	3,498.83	3,500.00	3.500.00
80	3,463.45	3,485.95	3,499.91	3,500.00
84	3,369.89	3,415.97	3,491.53	3,500.00
88	3,189.67	3,221.48	3,358.59	3,497.64
92	2.967.06	2,935.52	2,874.55	2,897.51
96	2,781.32	2,725.44	2,464.42	2,139.34
100	2,637.30	2,662.76	2,629.16	2,544.30
104	2,427.63	2,575.56	2,910.06	3,250.04
108	2,019.03	2,227.14	2,649.77	2,896.67
112	1,351.36	1,534.06	1,804.81	1,897.29
116	454.67	572.52	687.67	700.00
120	−597.17	−537.14	−500.89	−500.00
124	−1734.32	−1709.12	−1700.03	−1700.00

Index

Note: Page references in *italics* refer to Figures; those in **bold** refer to Tables

Index compiled by Annette Musker